15 Days of Prayer
With Saint Louis de Montfort

Also in the *15 Days of Prayer* collection:

Saint Teresa of Ávila

The Curé of Ars

Pierre Teilhard de Chardin

Saint Bernard

Saint Augustine

Meister Eckhart

Thomas Merton

Saint Benedict

Charles de Foucauld

Saint Francis de Sales

Johannes Tauler

Saint Dominic

Don Bosco

Saint Alphonsus Liguori

Saint John of the Cross

Saint Thérèse of Lisieux

Saint Catherine of Siena

Saint Bernadette of Lourdes

Saint Thomas Aquinas

15 DAYS OF PRAYER

WITH

Saint Louis de Montfort

VÉRONIQUE PINARDON AND JEAN BULTEAU

Translated by Victoria Hébert and Denis Sabourin

Liguori
LIGUORI, MISSOURI

Published by Liguori Publications
Liguori, Missouri
www.liguori.org
www.catholicbooksonline.com

This book is a translation of *Prier 15 Jours Avec Louis-Marie Grignon de Montfort,* published by Nouvelle Cité, 1996, Montrouge, France.

Library of Congress Cataloging-in-Publication Data

Pinardon, Véronique.
    [Prier 15 jours avec Louis-Marie Grignon de Montfort. English]
    15 days of prayer with Saint Louis de Montfort / Véronique Pinardon and Jean Bulteau ; [translated by] Victoria Hébert and Denis Sabourin.
        p. cm.
    Includes bibliographical references.
    ISBN 0-7648-0715-3 (pbk.)
    1. Grignion de Montfort, Louis-Marie, Saint, 1673–1716— Meditations. 2. Spiritual life—Catholic Church. I. Bulteau, Jean. II. Title.

BX4700.G83 P56 2001
269'.6—dc21   00–052013

Printed in the United States of America
05 04 03 02 01   5 4 3 2 1
First English Edition 2001

Table of Contents

How to Use This Book ▪ vii

A Brief Chronology of Saint Louis de Montfort's Life ▪ xv

Introduction ▪ xxi

Abbreviations Used in This Book ▪ xxv

1. Day One—I Have a Father Who Is Infallible ▪ 1

2. Day Two—Come to Me, I Want to Make You Happy ▪ 8

3. Day Three—Jesus Christ, Eternal Wisdom and Born of Mary ▪ 14

4. Day Four—The New Wine of the Holy Spirit ▪ 20

5. Day Five—Everything Comes Through Prayer ▪ 27

6. Day Six—The Authority of the Word of the Holy Spirit ▪ 34

7. Day Seven—To Jesus Through Mary ▪ 41

8. Day Eight—The Irrevocable Gift of Our Heart ▪ 48

9. Day Nine—To Give Everything to Mary, to Lose Oneself in Her ▪ 54

10. Day Ten—I Thank God a Thousand Times for Passing
    As a Poor Person ▪ 61

11. Day Eleven—The Loving Invention of the Eucharist ▪ 68

12. Day Twelve—To Make Our Lord Loved ▪ 74

13. Day Thirteen—To Give Us Proof of His Love,
    Wisdom Chose the Cross ▪ 80

14. Day Fourteen—Students of a Crucified God ▪ 87

15. Day Fifteen—The Rose Is the Queen of All Flowers, the
    Rosary Is the Rose of All Devotions ▪ 93

Bibliography ▪ 101

How to Use This Book

AN OLD CHINESE PROVERB, or at least what I am able to recall of what is supposed to be an old Chinese proverb, goes something like this: "Even a journey of a thousand miles begins with a single step." When you think about it, the truth of the proverb is obvious. It is impossible to begin any project, let alone a journey, without taking the first step. I think it might also be true, although I cannot recall if another Chinese proverb says it, "that the first step is often the hardest." Or, as someone else once observed, "the distance between a thought and the corresponding action needed to implement the idea takes the most energy." I don't know who shared that perception with me but I am certain it was not an old Chinese master!

With this ancient proverbial wisdom, and the not-so-ancient wisdom of an unknown contemporary sage still fresh, we move from proverbs to presumptions. How do these relate to the task before us?

I am presuming that if you are reading this introduction it is because you are contemplating a journey. My presumption is that you are preparing for a spiritual journey and that you have taken at least some of the first steps necessary to prepare for this journey. I also presume, and please excuse me if I am making too many presumptions, that in your preparation for the spiritual journey you have determined that you need a guide. From deep within the recesses of your deepest self, there was something that called you to consider Louis Marie de Montfort as a potential companion. If my presumptions are correct, may I congratulate you on this decision? I think you have made a wise choice, a choice that can be confirmed by yet another source of wisdom, the wisdom that comes from practical experience.

Even an informal poll of experienced travelers will reveal a common opinion; it is very difficult to travel alone. Some might observe that it is even foolish. Still others may be even stronger in their opinion and go so far as to insist that it is necessary to have a guide, especially when you are traveling into uncharted waters and into territory that you have not yet experienced. I am of the personal opinion that a traveling companion is welcome under all circumstances. The thought of traveling alone, to some exciting destination without someone to share the journey with does not capture my imagination or channel my enthusiasm. However, with that being noted, what is simply a matter of preference on the normal journey becomes a matter of necessity when a person embarks on a spiritual journey.

The spiritual journey, which can be the most challenging of all journeys, is experienced best with a guide, a companion, or at the very least, a friend in whom you have placed your trust. This observation is not a preference or an opinion but rather an established spiritual necessity. All of the great saints with whom I am familiar had a spiritual director or a confessor who journeyed with them. Admittedly, at times the saint might well have traveled far beyond the experience of their guide and companion but more often than not they would return to their director and reflect on their experience. Understood in this sense, the director and companion provided a valuable contribution and necessary resource.

When I was learning how to pray (a necessity for anyone who desires to be a full-time and public "religious person"), the community of men that I belong to gave me a great gift. Between my second and third year in college, I was given a one-year sabbatical, with all expenses paid and all of my personal needs met. This period of time was called novitiate. I was officially designated as a novice, a beginner in the spiritual journey, and I was assigned a "master," a person who was willing to lead me. In addition to the master, I was provided with every imaginable book and any other resource that I could possibly need. Even with all that I was provided, I did not learn how to pray because of the books and the unlimited resources, rather it was the master, the companion who was the key to the experience.

One day, after about three months of reading, of quiet and solitude, and of practicing all of the methods and descriptions of prayer that were available to me, the master called. "Put away the books, forget the method, and just listen." We went into a room, became quiet, and tried to recall the presence of God, and then, the master simply prayed out loud and permitted me to listen to his prayer. As he prayed, he revealed his hopes, his dreams, his struggles, his successes, and most of all, his relationship with God. I discovered as I listened that his prayer was deeply intimate but most of all it was self-revealing. As I learned about him, I was led through his life experience to the place where God dwells. At that moment I was able to understand a little bit about what I was supposed to do if I really wanted to pray.

The dynamic of what happened when the master called, invited me to listen, and then revealed his innermost self to me as he communicated with God in prayer, was important. It wasn't so much that the master was trying to reveal to me what needed to be said; he was not inviting me to pray with the same words that he used, but rather that he was trying to bring me to that place within myself where prayer becomes possible. That place, a place of intimacy and of self-awareness, was a necessary stop on the journey and it was a place that I needed to be led to. I could not have easily discovered it on my own.

The purpose of the volume that you hold in your hand is to lead you, over a period of fifteen days or, maybe more realistically, fifteen prayer periods, to a place where prayer is possible. If you already have a regular experience and practice of prayer, perhaps this volume can help lead you to a deeper place, a more intimate relationship with the Lord.

It is important to note that the purpose of this book is not to lead you to a better relationship with Louis Marie de Montfort, your spiritual companion. Although your companion will invite you to share some of their deepest and most intimate thoughts, your companion is doing so only to bring you to that place where God dwells. After all, the true measurement of a companion for the journey is that they bring you to the place where you need to be, and then they step back, out of the picture. A guide who brings you to the desired destination and then sticks around is a very unwelcome guest!

Many times I have found myself attracted to a particular idea or method for accomplishing a task, only to discover that what seemed to be inviting and helpful possessed too many details. All of my energy went to the mastery of the details and I soon lost my enthusiasm. In each instance, the book that seemed so promising ended up on my bookshelf, gathering dust. I can assure you, it is not our intention that this book end up in your bookcase, filled with promise, but unable to deliver.

There are three simple rules that need to be followed in order to use this book with a measure of satisfaction.

Place: It is important that you choose a place for reading that provides the necessary atmosphere for reflection and that does not allow for too many distractions. Whatever place you choose needs to be comfortable, have the necessary lighting, and, finally, have a sense of "welcoming" about it. You need to be able to look forward to the experience of the journey. Don't travel steerage if you know you will be more comfortable in first class and if the choice is realistic for you. On the other hand, if first class is a distraction and you feel more comfortable and more yourself in steerage, then it is in steerage that you belong.

My favorite place is an overstuffed and comfortable chair in my bedroom. There is a light over my shoulder, and the chair reclines if I feel a need to recline. Once in a while, I get lucky and the sun comes through my window and bathes the entire room in light. I have other options and other places that are available to me but this is the place that I prefer.

Time: Choose a time during the day when you are most alert and when you are most receptive to reflection, meditation, and prayer. The time that you choose is an essential component. If you are a morning person, for example, you should choose a time that is in the morning. If you are more alert in the afternoon, choose an afternoon time slot; and if evening is your preference, then by all means choose the evening. Try to avoid "peak" periods in your daily routine when you know that you might be disturbed. The time that you choose needs to be your time and needs to work for you.

It is also important that you choose how much time you will spend with your companion each day. For some it will be possible to set aside enough time in order to read and reflect on all the material that is offered for a given day. For others, it might not be possible to devote one time to the suggested material for the day, so the prayer period may need to be extended for two, three, or even more sessions. It is not important how long it takes you; it is only important that it works for you and that you remain committed to that which is possible.

For myself I have found that fifteen minutes in the early morning, while I am still in my robe and pajamas and before my morning coffee, and even before I prepare myself for the day, is the best time. No one expects to see me or to interact with me because I have not yet "announced" the fact that I am awake or even on the move. However, once someone hears me in the bathroom, then my window of opportunity is gone. It is therefore important to me that I use the time that I have identified when it is available to me.

Freedom: It may seem strange to suggest that freedom is the third necessary ingredient, but I have discovered that it is most important. By freedom I understand a certain "stance toward life," a "permission to be myself and to be gentle and understanding of who I am." I am constantly amazed at how the human person so easily sets himself or herself up for disappointment and perceived failure. We so easily make judgments about ourselves and our actions and our choices, and very often those judgments are negative, and not at all helpful.

For instance, what does it really matter if I have chosen a place and a time, and I have missed both the place and the time for three days in a row? What does it matter if I have chosen, in that twilight time before I am completely awake and still a little sleepy, to roll over and to sleep for fifteen minutes more? Does it mean that I am not serious about the journey, that I really don't want to pray, that I am just fooling myself when I say that my prayer time is important to me? Perhaps, but I prefer to believe that it simply means that I am tired and I just wanted a little more sleep. It doesn't mean anything more than that. However, if I make it mean more than that, then I can become discouraged, frustrated, and put myself into a state where I might more easily give up. "What's the use? I might as well forget all about it."

The same sense of freedom applies to the reading and the praying of this text. If I do not find the introduction to each day helpful, I don't need to read it. If I find the questions for reflection at the end of the appointed day repetitive, then I should choose to close the book and go my own way. Even if I discover that the reflection offered for the day is not the one that I prefer and that the one for the next day seems more inviting, then by all means, go on to the one for the next day.

That's it! If you apply these simple rules to your journey you should receive the maximum benefit and you will soon find yourself at your destination. But be prepared to be surprised. If you have never been on a spiritual journey you should know that the "travel brochures" and the other descriptions that you might have heard are nothing compared to the real thing. There is so much more than you can imagine.

A final prayer of blessing suggests itself:

Lord, catch me off guard today.
Surprise me with some moment of beauty
    or pain
So that at least for the moment
I may be startled into seeing that you are
    here in all your splendor,
Always and everywhere,
Barely hidden,
Beneath,
Beyond,
Within this life I breathe.

Frederick Buechner

REV. THOMAS M. SANTA, CSsR
LIGUORI, MISSOURI
FEAST OF THE PRESENTATION, 1999

A Brief Chronology of Saint Louis de Montfort's Life

EVER SINCE THE TIME of his beatification (in 1888) and especially since his canonization (in 1947), Saint Louis Marie Grignion de Montfort has had an astonishing influence on the Church. Even though his writings are likened to a "Catechism" of faith, it is his devotion to Mary which has spiked his popularity. Renewed interest in the Mother of Jesus has brought Louis de Montfort's writings and spirituality back to the forefront.

Often considered a "vagabond" for his seemingly controversial approach to spirituality and the practice of his faith during his lifetime, he was revered by numerous popes. It must be noted that Pope John Paul II has adopted Louis de Montfort's short "formula" of consecration— "Tuus Totus"—as his episcopal motto. This alone shows the high esteem in which he is held. John Paul II is quoted as saying that when he read his book, "True Devotion," it was a turning point in his life—he does not hesitate to quote him in his own encyclicals. Here is a short sketch of the major events in Louis Marie's life:

1673: Louis Marie Grignion is born to a poor family (his father was a notary—but he was known to take on many charity cases— what we would call "pro bono" work today) on January 31, the second of eighteen children (of which only a few survived their childhood), in the small village of Montfort, in the Brittany region of France. It is interesting to note that, in later years, he added "de Montfort" to his first names and dropped his family name. He stated that the reason for this was that he was so very touched by the place of his baptism (even though the family only stayed there just two years) that he felt it was more important to his spiritual history than his family name.

1674–1683:

Louis Marie and his family moved when he was two to a farm in the town of Iffendic, a few miles from Montfort. His father was generous but known for his temper, his mother for her deep piety. The family was practicing Catholics.

1684–1691:

Louis Marie was sent to Rennes (the capital of Brittany) to enroll in the Jesuit college there. His uncle, a priest, became one of his closest friends. Louis Marie was considered to be intelligent, studious, deeply religious, shy, as well as artistic.

His decision to enter the priesthood was made (as he tells us) at the Shrine of Our Lady in the Carmelite church in Rennes. He was already very devoted to the Blessed Virgin Mary.

1692–1699:

Louis Marie decided to continue his theological studies at the Saint Sulpice Seminary in Paris. Leaving the College in Rennes at age nineteen, he began a new chapter in his life: leaving everything up to Providence; joyously giving away all of his worldly goods to the poor. He begged for food and shelter on the road to Paris—total surrender to his Lord.

Once in Paris, he chose to live with the poor seminarians. He spent two years at the Sorbonne and six years with the Sulpicians. They branded him as "weak" because of his love for the poor and desire to serve those considered to be outcasts. He taught the Catechism to the poorest children in society.

He was given the job of librarian; this pleased him as he took great joy in reading the spiritual writings of such notables as Bernard of Clairvaux, Thomas Aquinas, Vincent de Paul, Francis de Sales, and Vincent Ferrer, just to name a few. Primarily a lover of the sacred Scriptures, they were, in his words, his "constant companion."

His goal was to become a missionary to the poor—in France or overseas—to proclaim the Good News of the Gospels to the marginalized of society, to speak to them of Jesus' love and about Mary, his mother.

1700–1705:

Louis Marie was ordained and celebrated his first Mass in the parish Church of Saint Sulpice on June 5, 1700 (his ministry would last a mere sixteen years).

He spent a few years with various missions, preaching parish renewals, as well as ministering to the destitute in the poorhouse in Poitiers (where he founded a congregation of women—the Daughters of Divine Wisdom, with Marie-Louise Trichet—who are devoted to the care of the destitute of society) and working with those who were both ill and poor at the General Hospital in Paris.

Opposition is so great that he is banned from preaching in Poitiers. He felt unfulfilled and sought a way to reach out to the poor with the Lord's message.

He decided to go to see the pope to ask for answers to his queries; to be able to go and be a missionary. He set out on foot from Poitiers, begging food and shelter on his way to the Holy City. Once he reached St. Peter's Basilica, he removed his sandals and immediately went to Peter's tomb.

1706–1709:

In June, he went to see the pope (Clement XI) and poured his heart out, explaining his plight and asking his counsel. The Holy Father saw him to be extraordinarily gifted and refused his request to "proclaim the Gospel in the wilds of Canada or in the Far East." Instead, he named him Apostolic Missionary, ordering him back to France to renew the Church there. Louis Marie returned to Poitiers on foot, conducting approximately 200 missions and retreats throughout Western France. He preached the devotion to Mary everywhere and to everyone. He preached against Jansenism.

1710–1714:

Yet another attempt was made on his life (poisoning) due to the style and contents of his preaching; this left him weakened. He had many enemies.

In an age when emphasis was placed on distancing God from the people, he sought to be like the poor, even recommending daily Communion and a total surrender to Jesus through Mary. The poor called him one of their own; he was known as the "good father with the big rosary." Many further attempts were made on his life, but this did not deter him from continuing his mission. He called himself "the loving slave of Jesus in Mary"—slave being understood in the New Testament sense as seen when Mary calls herself the slave girl of the Lord (see Lk 1:38) and as Paul calls himself the slave of Jesus (see Rom 1:1).

The Jesuits, Sulpicians, and Dominicans (which he joined—Third Order—in 1710) would, in the end, always be supportive.

This was a time of many "situations" for Louis Marie, some truthful, others not, which have been reported in various writings; these were trials of faith for him—trials when his faith was put to the ultimate test—refusals of support by bishops and friends alike. He said: "I have many friends...who love my hospitality, very few who love my cross" (LAC 11)—meaning that he had many "fair-weather" friends.

1715–1716:

In 1715, Louis Marie organized several priests and founded the Missionaries of the Company of Mary.

His health destroyed by pleurisy, and frail from his sixteen priestly vagabond years, Louis Marie died in 1716 at Saint-Laurent-sur-Sever, France, at the age of forty-three.

It is said that Louis Marie's greatest contribution to the Church are his writings and teachings about total self-consecration to Mary. This, for Louis Marie, was a way in which a believer could renew and fulfill his baptismal promises.

The cause for his declaration as a Doctor of the Church is currently under study. His feast day is April 28.

Introduction

LOUIS MARIE, "MASTER AND WITNESS"

To set aside, for fifteen days, a time for prayer with Saint Louis Marie is to become a student of both a master and a witness. John Paul II, in his encyclical entitled "The Mother of the Redeemer," invoking the "true Marian spirituality and corresponding devotion," wrote: "In this aspect, I like to highlight, amidst all of the witnesses and masters of this spirituality, the figure of Saint Louis Marie de Montfort who proposes that Christians consecrate themselves to Christ through Mary, as an efficient way to faithfully live out their baptismal promises" (no. 48).

Louis Marie is a master because of the quality of his teaching and the originality of the spiritual path that he proposes. He is a witness by means of the holiness of his life and the fruitfulness of his actions. At the same time both a mystic and a missionary, he knew to allow himself to be "molded" by Mary in order to become a living part of Jesus Christ, all the while teaching others to do the same.

There are two significant anecdotes which have been reported by one of his first biographers, Father Besnard, which illustrate the connection between his prayers and his actions. During the summer of 1707, when he was leading several retreats for lay people at the residence of the Sisters of the Cross, he was approached by someone who asked that he cut short his prayers. He replied: "Leave me alone (to continue my prayers), for if I am not good for myself, I will never be for others." A few months later, in Bréal (which is near Montfort), when the parish priest was surprised at the spiritual success of the mission, Louis Marie confided to him: "My dear friend, I have traveled two thousand miles on pilgrimages in order to ask God to grant me the grace to touch hearts. He has granted it."

FIFTEEN FACETS OF A UNIQUE GEM

Louis Marie always gave Jesus Christ preference. Throughout his entire life, he sought to know him. Having found him, he still sought him. He loved him above all else in the world and gave of himself without regard in order to make him known and loved. His preaching and writings map out a path of a characteristically Christian life. The diverse aspects of his spirituality are like the various facets of a unique gem. The Marian facet is the best known; there are also others. What is important, though, is the gem itself. For Louis Marie, this gem is Jesus Christ, the eternal Word, born of the Virgin Mary, true God and true man, who he was happy to call "the eternal and incarnate Wisdom of God" (see ASE). John Paul II understood the central place that Jesus Christ took in Montfort's spirituality. In his book, *On the Threshold of Hope*, he wrote: "Thanks to Saint Louis Marie Grignion de Montfort, I understood that authentic devotion to the Mother of God is truly *Christocentric*, profoundly rooted in the triune mystery and those of the Incarnation and Redemption."

We propose to present to you one of these "facets" of the unique gem that is Jesus Christ, in and through whom is made manifest both the Father and the Holy Spirit.

God the Father (day one) seeks man through love in order to communicate his life to him and make him happy (day two). He manifested himself in Jesus Christ, the Incarnate Wisdom of God, born of the Virgin Mary (day three) and who gave us the Holy Spirit (day four).

Prayer creates a desire in man for God and the capacity to welcome his love (day five). The Word of God (day six) and the Eucharist (day eleven) transform the image of the Son, little by little. God chose Mary as a means to come to us; it is through her also that we go to him, in Jesus Christ (day seven). In order to belong completely to Jesus Christ, with no reservations, and fully live our baptismal requirements (day eight), one must give oneself totally to Mary (day nine). Then one experiences the joy of being poor, of serving Jesus Christ amongst the poor (day ten), of proclaiming the immense love that Jesus Christ has for man and to make him loved (day twelve).

Love taken to the extremes, manifested by the choice of the cross (day thirteen), is a call to each disciple of Jesus to carry his own cross (day fourteen).

An expert in the art of reciting the rosary, Louis Marie could initiate us to it: the mysteries of the rosary, a summary of all that came before, makes us contemplate the love that both Jesus Christ and Mary had for all humanity and each one of us. They will make us part of their joys and sufferings, in the active expectation of sharing their glory (day fifteen).

A FEW COMMENTS

1. It is not necessary to follow the fifteen chapters in order, even if a certain logical progression links the chosen themes;

2. Let the Holy Spirit guide your prayers. Go with him. A single phrase or a single paragraph could suffice to nourish a prayer;

3. Louis Marie's message is a contemporary one, even if its dated language seems to lead one astray. In certain instances, some citations have been shortened, indicated as (...) without changing their meanings;

4. Louis Marie spoke often of "Wisdom." What he meant was either the Wisdom of God, personified in the Old Testament, or Jesus Christ himself (see ASE 13);

5. Certain voluntary repetitions could only assist a prolonged prayer lasting fifteen days.

Abbreviations Used in This Book

L   Letters

ASE   *The Love of Eternal Wisdom*

LAC   Letter to the Friends of the Cross

SAR   *The Admirable Secret of the Rosary*

MR   Methods of Reciting the Rosary

SM   *The Secret of Mary*

VD   *True Devotion to the Blessed Virgin*

PE   Burning Prayer (for Missionaries)

ACM   Letter to the Members of the Company of Mary

RS   The Rule of the Daughters of Wisdom

LM   Letter to the Inhabitants of Montbernage

C   Canticles (Hymns)

CA   A Contract of Covenant with God

OC   Complete Works (translated into English as *God Alone: The Collected Writings of St. Louis Marie de Montfort*)

DAY ONE

I Have a Father
Who Is Infallible

FOCUS POINT

Complete trust in God's will: that is the spiritual outlook Louis de Montfort took early in his life. When events in his life were good, or when they seemed not to be going his way, Louis abandoned himself to God's plan. In our own lives, this is wonderful spiritual practice. Events in our lives, whether we interpret them as "good" or "bad," always offer tremendous opportunities for us to grow in our love for God. They key is that, in all events, we remain open to God's will and allow that will to draw us closer to our heavenly Father.

Just like you gave me news of a death in your letter, I will also give you such news. Mr. de la Barmondière, my superior and director, who was so good to me here, has died.... It was he

*who founded the seminary where I am and who had the gener-
osity to accept me here for nothing. I do not yet know how
things will go, if I will stay or leave, for we have not yet found
his will. No matter what happens to me, I will not be embarrassed. I have a Father in heaven who is infallible. He led me
here, he has kept me up until now, and he will continue to do
so through his mercy. Since I merit nothing more than punishment for my sins, I never stop praying to God and abandoning
myself to his providence... (L 2, September 29, 1694, extract).*

L ouis Marie wrote this letter to his uncle, Father Alain Rob-
ert, when he was twenty-one years old and beginning his
second year of studies at the high seminary, living in a community with seminarians who had little or no financial means.
The death of his benefactor did not seem to bother him in the
least: he abandoned himself to God and his divine providence.

In the thirty-four letters he wrote (see OC), ten out of the
eleven that were written from September 1694 to July 1702
made reference to Providence. It was Providence that led him
to "the seminary of Saint Sulpice through contact with Ma-
dame d'Alègre" (L 3). It was Providence who took care of his
material needs (L 4). It was again Providence who used him
for missions or in service to the poor (L 10, 11). It was Providence who took his situation in hand when the need was there
(L 11). It was into the hands of Providence that he placed all
his worries (L 5). Nothing and no one could compel him to
separate himself from "Divine Providence, his Mother" (L 6).
"Mary, the inexhaustible treasure of the Lord...the treasurer
and dispenser of all of his gifts," (ASE 207) naturally had her
place close beside Providence (L 1, 7, 8, 9, 11).

This would be his attitude for his entire life. Three week before his death, he summed up his experiences by telling the people who were responsible for caring for the incurable patients at Nantes the following: "One must, whether for their greater or lesser good, through knowledge or ignorance, never lean on an arm made of flesh, nor on their natural talents, but uniquely on the invisible and unknown help of the divine providence of our heavenly Father" (L 33, April 4, 1716).

Louis Marie's motto, "God alone," was not just a passing phrase written on a piece of paper. It was a conviction of faith, the source and expression of his vital relationship and constant attitude towards God. His "Credo" was not abbreviated: he did not believe only in an all-powerful God, but in a God that is both Father and all-powerful, and "infallible," to whom he could totally abandon himself, and from whom he could expect everything (to come) with the confidence of a child.

Modern man, even a Christian, is less inclined to defer to God in all things, to see an active presence of the heavenly Father in his life. If he labels an unplanned and happy solution to a problem as "providential," he more often questions God when faced with the many manifestations of evil in the world: "What about him then, the all-powerful?" Or rather, he doubts that God is the Father: "If God was so good, that wouldn't happen."

Very early on, Louis Marie discovered the true face of God revealed in Jesus: "When you pray, say 'Father'" (Lk 11:2). "If you then, who are evil, know how to give good gifts to your children, how much more will the heavenly Father give the Holy Spirit to those who ask him!" (Lk 11:13).

Father, at my baptism you gave me your Holy Spirit. At the deepest part of me you confirm my position as a son and allow me to call you by your real name (see Gal 4:6). What a marvel! Teach me to remain speechless before you, in adoration, admiration, and filial praise, simply because you are the Father, my Father. I will want for nothing if I count on you. Open my being to the revelation of your Father's heart for each of your children.

I know you not only as my beginning, but also as the source from which continually flows my existence. I am the fruit of the inexhaustible, never-ending gift of your love. You create me constantly. It will be like this eternally.... Even at this very moment, I receive myself from you, from your love. I give you thanks.

Father, you are only love, you love me immensely, you can't go on without me. Your nature is to give, to give of yourself. You give eternally of yourself to your Son, and, through him, to each human. Your plan, as the Father, is to transmit your life to your children, to make each of them, freely, an heir to your happiness. Saint Paul understood it; I hear him tell me: "So you are no longer a slave but a child, and if a child, then also an heir, through God" (Gal 4:7). With all saints, past, present, and future, I offer my thanks for your love. Amen.

What a blessing it was for Louis Marie to realize, at a young age, that he had "a Father in heaven who is infallible." Even though his relationship with his earthly father had, at times, been strained, often unjustly, he knew that his heavenly Father was his All-Other. He abandoned himself totally to him.

However, this abandonment did not lead Louis Marie to passivity or inactivity. Throughout his entire life he wanted to "undertake and do great things" (VD 265, see ASE 61, 100). To wait to receive everything from God implies an active cooperation. Because he is love, God never imposes himself on anyone; he proposes, asks for freedom, and creates a free reply. God allows man to invent his life with him through the events of each day; just as he did with Jesus during his earthly existence. It is up to man to take the initiative and to decide for himself, all the while counting on God.

Isn't the tragedy of many people's lives the fact that they live without reference to God as the Father, either through ignorance, negligence, indifference, or a refusal to see it? Cut off from their source, they can only rely upon themselves. In the same way, they pay no attention to their destiny and find themselves at a dead end. Who will give meaning to their life? Who will tell them that they have an "infallible Father"?

Father, make yourself known (see Lk 11:2). Do it first to me so that I can throw myself into your arms like a child and so that I can cry out to my brothers that you love them all, each and every one, immensely.

Make me know you as the source of my existence, to welcome all that comes to me from you. If I first seek your kingdom and your justice, everything else will be given to me in surplus. I need not "worry about tomorrow, for tomorrow will bring worries of its own. Today's trouble is enough for today" (Mt 6:33–34). It's a crazy gamble on faith! The certainty of the revelation of your true face as God the Father in Jesus: you withdraw yourself before the creature, you show him the path without restricting him from walking there, you offer him the ability to realize his life, with you, for you are love.

The constant flow from the Father is not an invitation to laziness. God needs the responsible commitment of man after having made him a partner in creation.

And that often comes dearly! The invitation to ask for our daily bread from the Father doesn't erase the punishment of Genesis: "By the sweat of your face you shall eat bread..." (Gen 3:19). Even if Louis Marie expected to receive everything from Providence, he always did his share. It is thus that he never held back when he was needed to help anyone.

In the Rule of the Daughters of Wisdom, Louis Marie wrote: "...for everything they will abandon themselves to Divine Providence who will help them in the manner and time he pleases...; and nevertheless, they will perform manual labor in order to gain something, as if they expected nothing from God" (RS 29). He knew that everything comes from God and man at the same time.

Having lived with the Jesuits for eight years, in Rennes, perhaps he had been impregnated with the Ignatian tradition that a Hungarian member of the Company expressed, in 1705, in this paradoxical formula: "This is the first rule of action: trust in God as if the success of things completely depended upon God and nothing on you; then put all your labors into it as if God is going to do nothing and you everything."

I am your protection and your defense...the Eternal Father tells you, I have engraved you in my heart and written with my hands, to cherish you and defend you, because you have placed your trust in me and not in man, in my providence and not in money.... I will deliver you from the traps that await you, I will carry you on my shoulders, I will answer your prayers, I will accompany you in your suffering, I will deliver you from all evil (ACM 3).

REFLECTION QUESTIONS

When events occur in my life, do I have a tendency to group them as either "good" or "bad"? Does this delineation color my outlook on these events as their being either "grace-filled" or "godless"? How can my accepting God's will (and abandoning my own will) turn every event in my life into a grace-filled opportunity? Isn't it possible that God is available to me at every moment of my life if only I will open myself to his will and learn from every event—tragic or joyous, exciting or ordinary—I encounter?

DAY TWO

Come to Me,
I Want to Make You Happy

FOCUS POINT

The Lord is always calling us, calling us to a deeper union with him. Louis Marie recognized this in his own life, and always sought to draw closer and closer to God. It is God who initiates our longing for the Divine; God loves us into existence and instills within us a deep desire for happiness—a happiness we can truly experience only in God. From the beginning of creation, it was this way. And though we may be lost at times, seeking happiness in lesser goods than God, we are always called to the Source of our being, the goal of our life's pursuits: God.

There is such a great love connection between Eternal Wisdom and man that it is incomprehensible. Wisdom is (created) for man and man for Wisdom.... He is an infinite treasure for man.... This friendship between Wisdom and man comes from what he is, in creation, a summary of his (God's) marvels...his living image...and since, through an overabundance of love he brings to him, he has come to resemble him by making himself like man. Submitting himself to death in order to save man, he loves him like a brother, a friend, a disciple, a student, the prize for (the shedding of) his blood and the coheir to the kingdom, in such a way that he suffers infinitely when he is refused or loses heart. This eternally and sovereignly loving beauty has such a desire for man's love that he created a book just to win him, in it uncovering his excellence and the desire he has for him. This book is like a letter from one lover written to his love in order to gain its affection. The desire for the heart of man that he contains is so fervent, the searches for his love that he makes are so tender, the calls and wishes are so loving, that to hear about it, you would say that he could not be the Sovereign of heaven and earth and that he needed man to be happy. Sometimes, in order to find man, he runs along the main roads; at another, he climbs up to the highest summits of the mountains; yet, at another, he goes out to the limits of the cities; still yet at another, he goes all the way into the public places, right into the midst of public gatherings, crying out with the loudest voice that he can: "O men! O children of men! I have cried out to you for such a long time!...come to me; I want to make you happy" (ASE 64–66).

We meet the God with a human face through the writings of a witness to his love. At this point in time, a time that is full of potential, but ridden with risks, we sometimes feel dizzy when faced with a world where the force of a destructive spirit manifests itself so much and in so many different ways. We are touched in our righteous aspiration for a progression to and hope for happiness for humanity. And we could affirm that modern man, confronted with a culture of death, is concerned to, again, find wisdom for life.

Louis Marie presents Eternal Wisdom to us as a friendly kind of wisdom for man, and he invites us to desire, discover, and love him. May the Holy Spirit establish his dwelling within us and ease the tumult of our thoughts so that we can call upon and acquire him: "Oh! When will I possess this lovable and unknown wisdom? When will he come and dwell within me? When will I be sufficiently adorned to serve as a place of retreat for him when he is on the street and scorned!" (L 16). What, then is the object of his desire? Who, then, is this Wisdom? "Who only made himself become man in order to attract man's hearts to his love and imitation, who took pleasure in adorning himself with all of the lovability and the most charming human gentleness?" (ASE 117).

He is the one the world has not known and not accepted (see Jn 1:10–11). The Wisdom that Louis Marie offers us is, in fact, beyond all kinds of human wisdom. Inspired by the very Word of God in the Bible, he reveals Wisdom to us as a person who is gifted with a capacity of extraordinary feelings, for he is filled with divine Love. He calls Christ: "Eternal and Incarnate Wisdom," reminding us of a part of the mystery of his origins in God within the Trinity, a place of incessant exchange of love among the three divine Persons (see Jn 1:1); on the other hand, the loving presence of God in the creation. In other respects, he invites us to contemplate Christ, the Wisdom of God, the object of the Father's willingness, whose voice is heard in a cloud: "This is my Son, the Beloved; listen to him!" (Mk 9:7).

When Louis Marie fervently expressed Wisdom's bewildering tenderness for man, his ardent desire to reach him to make him happy, his desperate search to find him, approaching him in the fear that he would not be blown away by his amazing flash, waiting at the door of the one who arises in the morning in order to find him (ASE 69), it is his own conviction that he is expressing, but it is also the call for a passionate love that he wants to proclaim because it concerns everyone.

His message is addressed to each of us. We are all called to welcome this prodigy of the condescension of the Creator who makes the first move towards his creature, an incredible step that reveals the humility and discretion of a God who is respectful of our freedom as "sons and daughters." Therefore, let us desire, infinitely love, meet, and invite him to the feast, let us open our doors to the promised happiness: let us release the bonds and adore, for the mystery of the Wisdom of God is profound, immense, and incomprehensible. "O the depth of the riches and wisdom and knowledge of God! How unsearchable are his judgments and how inscrutable his ways!" (Rom 11:33). And Louis Marie makes this recommendation to us: "It is here that all spirits must negate themselves and adore, for fear of being oppressed by the immense weight of the glory of the divine Wisdom, by wanting to examine him" (ASE 15).

We can take the time to expose ourselves to this Wisdom of God through a meditation on his plan for the salvation of the world. His covenant with humanity, of which we are part, sealed in the dawn of time, was broken apart by sin, that of the first man, and by our own. Faced with this disaster, the divine heart, moved with sadness and overflowing with compassion, wanted to restore the condition of this man that he loved at any and all cost. He wanted to again find the son (or daughter) who was "lost" to sin. After the transgression, he left to seek him in Eden and his call, a tender whisper, was Adam, "where are you?" (Gen 3:9).

Let us listen to Louis Marie speak to us about the marvels of the bounty and mercy of Eternal Wisdom, which triumph over justice in the edict of the Incarnation at the great council of the Holy Trinity. "Eternal Wisdom is vividly touched by poor Adam's misfortune and that of his descendants. He sees, with great displeasure...his masterpiece destroyed.... He sees with compassion... (there are) tears in his eyes...pain in his heart..." (ASE 41). God awaits the plea of the suffering man and he wants to bring him near. How difficult it is for us to remain hopeful when the horizon appears dark, to believe that we are not alone when faced with our sin. With Louis Marie, we can pray the Our Father in order to express our confidence with his permanently loving presence at our side.

As God becomes "Emmanuel," the intensity of his love for man is revealed to us. It is a love that would last all the way to death (and beyond) in order to save us all. To this generosity that is beyond expression, of which we are made more conscious through the contemplation of the crucified Christ, what response would you like to give? We are invited to welcome his mercy without enclosing ourselves upon our weaknesses and frailties. "For the Son of Man came to seek out and to save the lost" (Lk 19:10). We could make ourselves part of his loving search with the poor and sinners in the same manner as did Louis Marie. With him, we can constantly ask for the grace to obtain Wisdom for ourselves and those we meet, a gift that is very precious, for "he wants to make us happy."

O God of my fathers, Lord of mercies, spirit of truth...prostrate before your divine majesty, recognizing the infinite needs I have for your divine Wisdom, which I lost through my sins, and confident of the infallible promise you made to those who will ask it of you without hesitation. Today, I ask it of you with all possible insistence, and the most profound humility; Lord, send us this Wisdom...to help our weakness, to enlighten our spirits, to inflame our hearts, to speak and act, to work and suffer along with you, to direct our steps, and to fill our souls with the virtues of Jesus Christ and the gifts of the Holy Spirit, since that is where all of your wealth is enclosed. O Father of mercies, O Father of all consolation, we ask you for the infinite treasure of your divine Wisdom, through the merciful womb of Mary, through the precious blood of your most dear Son, and through the extreme desire that you have to transfer your wealth to your poor creatures, answer my prayer. Amen (MR 11).

REFLECTION QUESTIONS

In what ways do I notice God calling me in my life? Do I hear God's call in nature? In the voices of my family and friends? In my deep desire to go outside of myself and seek something greater than myself? How do I respond to this divine call? Am I more open to those around me? Do I find myself (as Saint Ignatius Loyola did) "seeking God in all things"? Do I devote appropriate time in quiet to just being with God, open to his Word, conscious of his call?

DAY THREE

Jesus Christ, Eternal Wisdom and Born of Mary

FOCUS POINT

Mary is our spiritual mother, our great intercessor, and spiritual model. Mary's acceptance of God's will allowed her to be used as the perfect instrument of divine love: the pure vessel of the Incarnation. We pray to Mary to "pray for us sinners" so that we might be open to God's grace and all the wonderful acts he wills to work through us. We must abandon ourselves to God as Mary has done, so that God's will may be done on earth (and through us) as it is written in heaven.

Time constraints do not permit me to stop here to explain the excellence and grandeur of the mystery of Jesus who lives and reigns in Mary, or that of the Incarnation of the Word. I will content myself to say, in just a few words, that the first mys-

tery of Jesus Christ is here: it is the most hidden, the most revealed and least known. In this mystery, Jesus, in concert with Mary, in her womb, which is called God's secret room, the chosen people are selected; it is in this mystery that all the other mysteries that followed in his life operate through the acceptance that occurred there; and, consequently, this mystery is a summary of all the other mysteries, enclosing the will and grace of all; so that this mystery is the throne of mercy, generosity, and glory of God... (VD 248).

Jesus Christ is the Incarnate Word: eternally engendered in the bosom of the Father, conceived of the Holy Spirit, and born of the Virgin Mary. The Incarnation was the decisive moment in the history of salvation. By making himself become "flesh" (Jn 1:14) in the womb of a woman, the Word began to exist in the human condition. The eternal Word and the Jesus of history are one unique identical person, hereafter in two natures: "Eternal Wisdom in eternity or Jesus Christ in (human) time" (ASE 13). "O Eternal and Incarnate Wisdom, true God and true man, only Son of the eternal Father and of Mary, ever virgin! I profoundly adore you in the womb and splendors of your Father, for all eternity, and in the virginal womb of Mary, your very noble Mother, at the time of your Incarnation" (ASE 223).

The Incarnation manifests the immense love that God has for man. It reveals his "generosity," his "compassion," and his "mercy," his need to continue to inspire life, while man chose death, and his determination to "repair his destroyed masterpiece." The Father and the Holy Spirit are naturally associated with the Word in this enterprise. Since the beginning, all three of them shared the same infinite tenderness towards man. The Word, "revealed in flesh" (1 Tim 3:16), provides eloquent witness to this fact. This tenderness leads Jesus to the "relinquishment of his life" through death on the cross.

Louis Marie insists on the exceptional place given to Mary through the realization of the salvific plan. "God the Father gave his only Son to the world uniquely through Mary." He gave her "the power to produce his Son and all of the members of his Mystical Body" (VD 16–17). "The Son of God made himself man for our salvation, but in and through Mary." He wanted to depend upon her: He "found his freedom by being contained in her womb…" (see VD 16–19). God the Holy Spirit formed Jesus Christ in Mary, but after having asked for her consent. He made her his "beloved and indissoluble Spouse": "With her, in her, and of her he produced his masterpiece, who is a God made man, and whom he produces every day until the end of the world…the members of the Body of this adorable Head" (see VD 16, 20, 21). Just as God never changes, the place that has been made for Mary in the Incarnation remains and will remain the same until the return of Jesus Christ.

Mary's freely-given consent had been necessary. The Incarnation is the result of two "yes" responses. First, it was Jesus' "yes": "when Christ came into the world, he said: 'sacrifices and offerings you have not desired, but a body you have prepared for me…. Then I said, *See, God, I have come to do your will…*'" (Heb 10:5–7). Then there was Mary's "yes." She said to the angel: "Here I am, the servant of the Lord; let it be with me according to your word" (Lk 1:38).

Following these two "yes" responses, there is to be a "yes" from each baptized person so that Christ can continue "to incarnate himself every day…in his members" (VD 31). Supported by God's loving initiative, the personal agreement of man remains indispensable. In fact, God proposes and man disposes! Only in heaven will we measure the fruitfulness of our simple "yes" responses and the sterility of our refusals.

Acquiescent to the angel's proposition, Mary became the Mother of God, the Mother of Christ and of "all the members of his Mystical Body." In his flesh, the Word took on a body. It was the beginning of the new creation, that of the new man. At the same time, it was a physical and a spiritual maternity which, together, established an unutterable connection between Mary and the "fruit of her womb." What a sublimely great expression of God's condescension! The "most hidden" mystery, the "least known," a mystery of reciprocal intimacy, a mystery of love. "There is never and will never be a creature where God would be greater, outside of himself and within himself, than in...Mary. Mary is God's paradise, where the Son entered in order to make marvels. God is everywhere, but there is no point of connection where creatures could find themselves closer to her, or more adapted to his weakness than in Mary..." (see SM 19, 20). What faith was required of Mary, at the Annunciation and throughout her existence, to recognize her God, first as a fetus in her womb, since that is the reality of Incarnation, then as a child, an adolescent, and then as a simple worker in the village...waiting to "become" bread to be eaten. "We only see God through faith" (C 6, 5). "The blessed Virgin is truly praised / For her faith in the Lord/ It is faith that consecrated her! The Mother of her Creature" (C 6, 22).

Happy are you, Mary, to have "heard" the Word of God and believed it: you welcomed the Word into your heart before conceiving it in your body. Your faith "had been greater...than the faith of all the patriarchs, prophets, apostles, and all the saints" (VD 214). Through you, "God foresaw better for us": leaving what was secure, you told him "yes," without knowing where, or on what road he was leading you. Abraham's faith made him become the father of many; your faith made you the Mother of God, the Mother of the Church—the believers—and the Mother of all humanity. Your "yes" allowed the Holy Trinity to manifest his infinite tenderness and save man by offering a body to the incarnate Word.

Assist me and all of your children to be "wise" enough to believe as you believed. "Worthy Mother of God / Pure and faithful Virgin / Impart your faith to me / I will have Wisdom through her / And all men will come to me" (C 124, 8).

The Incarnation, the consequence of Mary's faith and her unconditional reply to God through love, plainly reveals Mary's vocation to us, her place in God's plan: Mary had no other reason for being than Jesus, in him and in his members. Between the Son and his Mother there is an "intimate union." "They are so intimately united that one is everything in the other: Jesus is completely in Mary, and Mary, completely in Jesus; or rather, she no longer exists except in Jesus; and we would rather separate the light from the sun than Mary from Jesus. It is so much so that we can call our Lord, Jesus of Mary, and the Blessed Virgin, Mary of Jesus" (VD 247). It is in this way that she continues to be closely associated to the salvific mission of her son: "It is through the Most Blessed Virgin that Jesus Christ came to the world and it is also through her that he will reign in the world" (VD 1). Just like the Son incarnates himself through her by the Holy Spirit, all of the children of God continue to be incarnated through her and in her. It is up to us to establish a filial relationship with Mary and allow her to give birth to us to the divine life.

O Mother of mercy! Give me the grace to obtain the true Wisdom of God and count me amongst those whom you love, teach, lead, nourish, and protect as one of your children....

O faithful Virgin, in all things, make me a perfect disciple of incarnate Wisdom, Jesus Christ, your son. May I reach, through your intercession, following your example, the plenitude of his time on earth and his glory in heaven (ASE 227).

REFLECTION QUESTIONS

How do I seek to make my will more malleable to God's divine plan? Do I devote time to silent prayer so that I might become more aware of what God is calling me to do? Do I fast regularly so that my physical hunger will move my spiritual hunger in the direction of the banquet of heaven and cause my focus to narrow on the will of God? Do I deny myself simple pleasures from time to time so that I may know what it means to go without, and to rely on God's goodness and grace to a greater degree?

DAY FOUR

The New Wine
of the Holy Spirit

FOCUS POINT

When one is intoxicated by the new wine of the Holy Spirit, one seems a fool in the eyes of the world. But this intoxication is an enlightenment; it allows one to see with new eyes, with eyes of faith. One can see and feel the importance of God's abiding love; one knows to what end one must direct one's life and one's will. Anything less than God will not suffice, will not feed the soul's hunger. A strong devotion to Mary welcomes the Holy Spirit into the soul, as the Spirit always feels at home with the Blessed Virgin.

What am I asking of you? Priests free of your freedom, detached from everything.... Men according to your heart who, without their own will, do what you wish.... Clouds above the earth full of heavenly dew which, without barriers, fly at will according to the breeze of the Holy Spirit. It is those, in part, of whom your prophets had knowledge when they asked: "Who are these that fly like a cloud?" (Isa 60:8). "Each moved straight ahead; wherever the spirit would go, they went..." (Ezek 1:12). People always available to you, always ready to run and suffer everything with you and for you, like the apostles: "Let us go, that we may die with him" (Jn 11:16). True children of Mary, your holy Mother, who would be engendered and conceived through her charity, enriched with her graces (PE 7–11).

Louis Marie was welcoming to the Holy Spirit and led by the Holy Spirit whose action manifested himself as powerful and unforeseeable in his life and through the long-lasting aspect of his work. At the end of his life, in a letter which is referred to as "a last breath from his heart," Louis Marie wrote to Marie-Louise Trichet: "If God hadn't given me eyes other than those given to me by my parents, I would complain, I would be worried like the fools in this corrupt world. But I am far from doing that" (L 34). He feared nothing in the foolishness of the world. But his temperament and his grace brought him to the foolishness of Wisdom, the one that Paul spoke of when he said: "Those who are unspiritual do not receive the gifts of God's Spirit, for they are foolishness to them, and they are unable to understand them because they are spiritually discerned. Those who are spiritual discern all things, and they are themselves subject to no one else's scrutiny" (1 Cor 2:14–15). Louis Marie was spiritual. His co-disciple and friend at the seminary, Mr. Blain, wrote: "I believe that I have the power to say that he thus feels the strength and the impetuosity of the new wine of the Holy Spirit, which made the apostles seem foolish and senseless to man's eyes, while they were wise in the eyes of God."

What, then, is this gaze which Louis Marie calls gratified? He had eyes that saw further than those he received at birth, that saw beyond human realities by grasping the mysterious signs of the Holy Spirit? Without a doubt, he was chosen and possessed by the Holy Spirit who had become his own spirit. He let himself be touched by the loving call of Eternal Wisdom: he desired, sought, welcomed, and delivered himself to him and Wisdom found him to be worthy. He wrote: "This sovereign beauty, being naturally a friend to goodness... particularly to man's well-being, his greatest pleasure is to manifest himself to man. That is why the Holy Spirit said that he seeks, spreads, and transports himself into holy souls" (ASE 90). Thus, Louis Marie places himself in the lineage of Moses, Solomon, Jacob, the Doctors of the Church, the apostles, and the prophets. And when he speaks to us about the marvelous effects produced in the soul of those who possess him, it is his own personal experience he is revealing and we have a great deal to learn from it.

Right away, we can stop and look at this characteristic of "worthiness" that is necessary for communication of the Spirit of Wisdom. Who, then, is worthy? Who, then, is holy? Who, then, can receive all of the benefits that he holds in his hands? "All good things came to me along with her, and in her hands uncounted wealth" (Wis 7:11). The word "worthiness" has lost all of its meaning. It corresponds to the writer's era, where the idea of transcendence was much more present in Christianity than that of proximity. Let us understand it to mean that Wisdom seeks people who are living under the movement of the Holy Spirit, freeing themselves of a nature that was spoiled by excessive self-love, by converting their passions, and uniting themselves to the incessant complaint that sighs in their hearts. "Likewise the Spirit helps us in our weakness; for we do not know how to pray as we ought, but that very Spirit interceded with sighs too deep for words. And God, who searches the heart, knows what is the mind of the Spirit, because the Spirit intercedes for the saints according to the will of God" (Rom 8:26–27). Let us invoke the Holy Spirit with Louis Marie: "Come Father of lights, formulate our prayers within us.... Into our souls make descend / A coal from your fire / which penetrates them with the flame / And fill them with God" (C 141, 1).

Louis Marie makes us notice the discretion of the interventions by Wisdom which reaches from one extremity to another with strength and disposes of everything with gentleness. His action is gentle, without any violence (see ASE 53). It is an invitation for us to put ourselves into the hands of Wisdom, to let ourselves be led by his Spirit. It assures us that Wisdom works in us, unbeknownst to us, often in a way that is so secret we don't even know it. He spreads his Spirit of light into the one who possesses him, and the knowledge that he gives is enlightening, moving, and pleases the heart by illuminating the spirit (see ASE 91, 92, 94).

Louis Marie received this gift of Wisdom in an eminent degree. He found its source in his famished search, through his incessant prayer, and fulfills himself in Mary. Even at a young age, he said that he would become "an old man in enlightenment, holiness, experience, and wisdom" (VD 156). He intensely perceived the special connection between the Holy Spirit and Mary. Assuredly, for him, the Holy Spirit was God in this divine Person, who is all relationships and communication in the midst of the Trinity, who is, mysteriously, love. But this love, so imperceptible, made a particular choice in the person of Mary. "It is with her, and in her, and of her that he produced his masterpiece which is God made man" (VD 20). He had the conviction that the Holy Spirit was pleased to act with her, for there was an affinity between them, an attraction, a natural complaisance. "When the Holy Spirit...finds her in a soul, he flies there" (VD 36). To those who throw themselves completely into Mary in order to be molded by the Holy Spirit, he recommended absolute poverty, self-abandonment without reservation, radical disapprobation, a complete voiding which frees from the spirit of the created world in order to make one available to Christian newness. If we want to do it, we can adopt these spiritual attitudes and live, "giving it all up" to Mary's hands.

Who doesn't get the grace of the Holy Spirit, offered to man by God, when he received it through Mary and welcomed in Mary? "God the Holy Spirit gave Mary, his faithful spouse, his unutterable gifts, and he chose her as the dispenser of all that he possessed" (VD 25). Louis Marie, who was "born for action," lived a mystical relationship with Mary. In her, he found the most sure way to deliver himself totally to Wisdom and to efficiently work for the extension of the kingdom of God. "Just as if there was nothing more active than Wisdom, those who have his love are inflamed; Wisdom inspires them to great things for the glory of God and the salvation of souls" (ASE 100). Thus, he walks in the footsteps of the first disciples, of these uncertain men locked behind their walls, that the Holy Spirit of the Pentecost frees from their fears, and who will go out and proclaim the marvels of God.... He is also in a hurry to let the Holy Spirit play with human limitations, to hear God's plan and to participate in its realization. Intoxicated "with the new wine of the Holy Spirit," "foolish and senseless in the eyes of man," he cries out with all of his being and all of his actions about God's impatience for everything to be fulfilled in Christ. "He had made known to us the mystery of his will, according to his good pleasure that he set forth in Christ, as a plan for the fullness of time, to gather up all things in him, things in heaven and things on earth" (Eph 1:9–10).

The breeze of the Holy Spirit blew on Louis Marie, and this man who "came from the wind" would pose prophetic gestures and, just as Wisdom is an invincible force, he makes everything imperceptibility and strongly come to his end by ways that are unknown to man (see ASE 5). We can remember the story of the foundation of the Daughters of Wisdom with Marie-Louise Trichet in Poitiers when the Mother Superior feared "that she would go crazy like that priest from the hospital." With and through Mary, "Wisdom has built his house" (see Prov 9:1). It is foolishness in the eyes of man, but Wisdom in God's eyes! Today, the universe is in a state of constant change—not always positive! The Spirit of Wisdom, always present and active, directs the cosmos towards its complete fulfillment in Christ. All Christians are called to this divine work. With and like Louis Marie, we will know nothing other than Jesus Christ (see 1 Cor 2:2). May we be able to become the children of God and Mary, and inebriate ourselves with "the new wine of the Holy Spirit," at the risk of allowing ourselves to become crazy with the Wisdom of God.

With Mary's spirit which is the Spirit of God, because she is always driven by the Spirit of God (see VD 258), let us pray:

Holy Spirit, remember to produce and form the children of God with your divine and faithful spouse, Mary. You formed the Head of the chosen ones with and in her; it is with and in her that you must form all his members. It is you alone who formed all of the divine persons outside of the Divinity, and all of the saints who have been and will be until the end of the world are as the many fruit of your love united to Mary.

The special reign of God the Father lasted until the deluge and had been terminated by a deluge of water; the reign of Jesus Christ had been terminated by a deluge of blood, but your reign, Spirit of the Father and the Son, continues right to the present and will be terminated by a deluge of fire, love, and justice.

When will this deluge of the fire of pure love that you must light across the whole earth happen? Send this Spirit of fire onto the earth, in order to create priests who will all be afire, through the ministry of whom the face of the earth will be renewed... (PE 15–17).

REFLECTION QUESTIONS

In what ways do I welcome the Holy Spirit into my life? How am I fostering a devotion to Mary? Do I pray the rosary on a regular basis? Do I attend novenas when I am able to? Do I attend Marian Masses on Saturdays? Am I welcoming the Holy Spirit into my life by devoting periods of silence to an awareness of God's presence and abiding love? Do I pray regularly that I might be graced to receive the precious gifts of the Holy Spirit?

DAY FIVE

Everything Comes Through Prayer

FOCUS POINT

For Louis Marie, there was a cyclical relationship between prayer and desire for Wisdom (God). Each one feeds off of the other, so the more a person prays, the more one desires Wisdom, and the more a person desires Wisdom, the more one prays. Prayer must be a constant in a person's life; one must never be discouraged in their spiritual life to the degree that they cease praying. It is especially during the dry spells in our spiritual life that we must pray with the most vigor.

The greater a gift from God is, the more difficult it is to obtain. What prayers, then, and what works do not require the gift of Wisdom, who is the greatest of all of God's gifts?

Let us listen to what Wisdom says: "Seek and you will find, knock and we will open it for you, ask and we will give it to you" (see Mt 7:7–11). It is as if Wisdom said: if you want to find me, you must seek me; if you want to enter my palace, you must knock at my door; if you want to receive me, you must ask. No one will find me unless he seeks me, no one will enter my home unless he knocks at my door; no one will obtain me unless he asks for me, and everything comes through prayer.

Prayer is the ordinary channel by which God gives his graces, particularly his Wisdom.... Solomon received it only after having asked for it for a long time, with a marvelous ardor: I address myself to the Lord, I make this prayer to him, I say it with my whole heart: Give me this Wisdom, the one who sits by your throne! (see Wis 8:21; 9:4). If any one of you needs Wisdom, ask God for him in all abundance...it will be given (see Jas 1:5) (ASE 184).

I t is God who first seeks man in order to make him happy. He waits at the door and knocks. He ardently wants man to hear his voice and opens the door to him in order to include him in the intimacy of his trinitarian love: "I will come in to you and eat with you, and you with me" (Rev 3:20). Man's eternal happiness is, therefore, God's hope, his most vivid desire.

God-Love's fundamental attitude towards his creature is to seek, ask, and find. It is also a necessity for man faced with his Creator and Father if he wants to give meaning to his life and realize it. No "foreign god" (Deut 32:12) could fulfill his heart. But the meeting that is always available to man depends upon man. If he closes himself upon himself, or if he is satisfied with the ephemeral, God's much-desired meeting will never happen. "Until when, children of men, will you have a heavy heart that is turned towards the earth? Until when will you continue to love vanity? Why not turn your eyes and hearts towards divine Wisdom, who, of all things that we could desire, is the most desirable; who, in order to make himself loved by man, unveils his origin, shows his beauty, displays his treasures and shows them in a thousand ways, how much he wants man to desire and seek him. He goes before those who desire him. We must be men of desire in order to have this great treasure of Wisdom" (ASE 181, 183).

To desire Jesus Christ (Wisdom), to find, possess, and inspire, with others, "a new desire to love him" (ASE 1), has always been Louis Marie's essential preoccupation, the unifying force of his life.

The quality of his prayer is an indicator of the intensity of his desire. This desire is strong and sincere; it is not a simple inclination: Louis Marie espoused Wisdom and took him as his lifelong "companion" (ASE 183). He gave himself totally to Wisdom; he wanted to do nothing to displease him. No other person would have such a place in his life. He invites us to do the same thing: "Jesus Christ...is everything that you could and must desire...he is this unique and precious gem for which you should be ready to sell all you have in order to acquire.... Desire and seek him..." (ASE 9). Always search for the one to whom we give preference once and for all.

To pray is to keep the door open to Jesus Christ, imploring him to enter and allowing him to establish a unique relationship of intimacy, communion, and love with us. In his Canticle 103, the expression "come into me" comes up fifty-six times like an instant supplication: "Son of God, supreme beauty / Come into me...O Word equal to his Father / Come into me...Jesus, uncreated Wisdom / Come into me...Jesus, Incarnate Wisdom / Come into me...You seek a dwelling / Come into me. Hasten, at any hour / Come into me...I have desired you a thousand times / Come into me. Without you, I suffer as a martyr / Come into me. With you, everything will be good for me / Without the fear of missing anything." The first words of the canticle give the key to this ardent litany: "Pardon me, divine Wisdom / For my ardor / For you are the Master / Of all of my heart." What loving passion he has for Jesus Christ, Wisdom! It is a never-ending passion, reached during long hours of meeting and contemplation: the desire for God brings about and supports prayer and prayer stirs up desire.

To pray is to keep oneself in the presence of God in reciprocal communication, in view of a communion; it is to listen to God revealing himself to man and unveiling his salvific plan; it is to welcome this salvation and respond to it by accepting the concrete requirements of love. It is an unutterable plan between the Creator and his creation, between the Father and his child. It is adoration, astonishment, admiration, praise, thanksgiving, and a silence of heart that allows itself to love and fulfill.

To recognize oneself as a sinner in the light of such love is neither humiliating nor destructive. Certainly, I am a sinner, but I am always a child of God, of a Father who is infinitely good and who loves me so much that he doesn't want to lose me (see Lk 15). I only have to cower and say: "Wash me thoroughly from my iniquity, and cleanse me from my sin...restore to me the joy of your salvation" (Ps 51:2, 12). "O Wisdom, come, the poor beg you" (C 124, 1). Thus I must not begin by looking at myself, but by forgetting myself, "voiding" or "renouncing" myself, disencumbering my heart in order to leave all of the room there for the One whom I welcome into myself.

Wisdom is not less than the All-Other; dwell in his presence, the terms "find" and "possess" him have nothing to do with a sentimental meeting. Louis Marie experienced being poor which stunned him and, without fear, bothered him: "God...wanted to be bothersome" (ASE 189). Hence, he advises us to, first, demand with a faith that is vivid and firm, without hesitation; for the person who has a faith that is wavering shouldn't expect to obtain the Wisdom of Jesus Christ (see ASE 185). And secondly, with a pure faith, without basing our prayer on sentimental consolation (see ASE 186), even if the one who prays has the impression "that God has no eyes to see his poverty, no ears to hear his requests...no hands to help him; whether he is attacked with distractions, doubts, and shadows of the spirit, with illusions in the imagination, with repugnance and worries of the heart, sadness, and agonies in the soul...the more faith we have, the more wisdom we have; the more wisdom we have, the more faith" (ASE 187).

"Thirdly, we must ask for Wisdom with perseverance." To get discouraged and stop praying is to "do wrong to God, who only wants to give, who always answers well-made prayers, in one way or another...through pure mercy, just like alms," freely (ASE 188).

Such a prayer purifies the heart and, little by little, leads it to love God for himself and to consider Jesus Christ as "the only good who will suffice for us" (VD 61). Prayer must also reach into the most intimate part of the heart of God, the Father and Savior of all mankind. It becomes a missionary commitment. Louis Marie prayed constantly, along his travels, at shrines and during hermitages. He said that it was a way to be "good to himself." He added "If I am not good to myself, I will not be for others." He asked God to be a "bearer of fruit" (see Jn 15:16). "I have traveled two thousand miles to ask for the grace to touch men's hearts and it was given to me."

In his long prayer (a dozen pages), in which he asked for missionaries, he spoke to God with a great familiarity, bewildering confidence, and total abandonment of himself. We can unite our supplication for the Church to a portion of his prayer:

> O great God, who can make so many children of Abraham out of rough stones, say a single word...in order to send good workers on your mission and good missionaries into your Church? (PE 3).
>
> Are you always quiet? Do you always suffer? Must your will not be done on earth as it is in heaven and must your kingdom not come? (PE 5).
>
> It is for your Mother that I pray to you.... Remember whose Son you are and answer me, remember what she is to you and what you are to her and satisfy my wishes. What am I asking you? Nothing for myself, everything for your glory. What am I asking? Something you can and even, I dare say, should grant me, like the true God you are, to whom all strength has been given on earth and in heaven, and like the best of all the children who infinitely love your Mother (PE 6).

He ends with this reprimand:

> Lord, wake up! Why do you pretend that you are sleeping? Awaken your strength, your mercy, and your justice...so that there is only one flock and one pastor, and that they all render you glory...Amen. God alone! (PE 30).

REFLECTION QUESTIONS

Do I experience dry periods in my prayer life? Am I discouraged in my prayer life because of this dryness? Might this dryness be a sign from God that I am ready to enter into a deeper union with him? Dry periods in one's prayer life are wonderful opportunities to grow in love with God; perseverance in one's practice of prayer is necessary during these times. Might I pray for God's grace that I persevere through difficult periods in my prayer life?

DAY SIX

The Authority of the Word of the Holy Spirit

FOCUS POINT

There is tremendous value in the Word of God, the sacred Scripture. Louis Marie recognized this great benefit of Scripture in his spiritual life, and we can seek its fruits in our own. There is inspiration to be found in each and every word of Scripture; in every corner of that holy text we find guidance and truth as we try to live our lives aware of God's abiding love. We are strengthened in our resolve to serve God and love others by the continual practice of reading the Word of God and applying it to our lives.

Here is the idea that the Holy Spirit, in order to conform to our weakness, gives us in the Book of Wisdom that he wrote just for us:

For Wisdom is a breath of the power of God, and a pure emanation of the glory of the Almighty; therefore, nothing defiled gains entrance into him. For he is the reflection of eternal light, a spotless mirror of the working of God, and an image of his goodness (see Wis 7:25–26).

It is the idea of divine beauty that was shown to Saint John the Evangelist when he cried: "In the beginning was the Word— or the Son of God or Eternal Wisdom—and the Word was with God, and the Word was God" (Jn 1:1).

About it, it is said that Wisdom had been created before all things: "Ages ago I was set up, at the first, before the beginning of the earth" (Prov 8:23).

It is from this beauty that God the Father took his pleasure for eternity and all time: "This is my Son, the Beloved; with him I am well pleased…" (Mt 17:5).

It is this enlightened brightness in which the apostles saw a few rays…which penetrated them with gentleness….

I have no words to explain the only impression that I have of this beauty…. Who could have a proper idea and explain it properly? Only you, great God, who knows what (the truth) is, could reveal it to whom you will (ASE 16–19).

I n his introduction to *The Love of Eternal Wisdom*, Louis Marie shares, with us, his prayer to Wisdom, which serves as a dedication to his book. Then he comments that he relinquishes to the authority of the words of the Holy Spirit: "My dear reader, I did not want to mix the shortcomings of my language with the authority of the words of the Holy Spirit" (ASE 5). He recognized the sacred aspect of the Scriptures by

proclaiming that he would follow Solomon's example:
"Solomon stated that he would give a faithful and exact de-
scription of Wisdom, and neither envy nor pride, which are
contrary to charity, will prevent him from transferring the
knowledge that has been given to him from heaven.... It is
after the example of this great man that I will simply explain
what Wisdom is and the ways to obtain it and keep it" (ASE
7).

Louis Marie had always respected and given value to the
Word of God. Even as a child, he would go to Church just to
be in the presence of God. During his schooling, he integrated
the Gospels into his thinking, to his own language. He took to
heart Paul's "charge" to Timothy: "But as for you, continue in
what you have learned and firmly believed, knowing from
whom you learned it, and how from childhood you have known
the sacred writings that are able to instruct you for salvation
through faith in Christ Jesus. All Scripture is inspired by God
and is useful for teaching, for reproof, for correction, and for
training in righteousness, so that everyone who belongs to God
may be proficient, equipped for every good work" (2 Tim 3:14–
17). He, who so ardently desired to know, love, and possess
Wisdom, ravishingly gathered Paul's conviction: the holy Scriptures could communicate Wisdom. If we seek Wisdom, we could
ask ourselves: what price would we be willing to place on the
Word of God? What time would we take to meditate on it, in
order to let it ripen, and verify how we put it into practice in
our lives?

With Louis Marie, we can ask to be allowed to recognize
the divine inspiration from the Bible. A few testimonies could
make it easier for us to grasp the honor which Louis Marie
accorded to the holy book and the role it played in his life. He
went on the road: "leaving everything to Providence, carrying

only the holy Bible, his breviary, a crucifix, his rosary, an image of the Blessed Virgin, and a walking stick with him."

This Word of God, welcomed into a heart vibrating with love, and ripened through the silence of contemplation would suggest an original and vibrant spiritual theology to Louis Marie. *The Love of Eternal Wisdom* is the most biblical of his writings. The reading of the Word that he gives us in it is a mystical approach driven by an intimate spiritual experience. Years of study and meditation had prepared the author for this text. But these pages also reflect his life, suffering, prayer, and his meeting with Wisdom. It is remarkable that it was probably written during his stay in Paris, when he experienced a time of extreme deprivation at Salpêtrière (1702–1704). At that time, he lived a time of personal sacrifice under the stairs of a wretched hovel near Saint Sulpice, when he could, at his ease, reflect, meditate, contemplate on, and commit himself to the vocation that was his: to speak about Wisdom. Louis Marie makes us understand that the Word of God, and that alone, could weigh heavily in situations that are humanly unsupportable. Contemporary people have given witness to this. Is this not an invitation to seek the light we need to help us make the difficult journeys of life in the Bible?

Louis Marie felt called to this special vocation of possessing Wisdom and speaking of it. In effect, he is truly the only spiritualist to have based his doctrine on the Book of Wisdom. He closely follows its progression, reproducing entire chapters, but, above all, he enters into a dynamic of interior movement. And he even goes above and beyond it by exposing the theme of the Incarnation, flooding the sapient vein with the fulfillment of Jesus Christ. When we browse through *The Love of Eternal Wisdom*, we are struck by and marvel at the charm that Wisdom exerts over the author: his "lovable prince." He wants to speak of his grandeur, beauty, and gentleness because he has personally tasted each of these and feels that it is his responsibility to tell the world. If he uses and quotes the Word of God, in spite of the "shadows of his spirit" and "the impurities of his mouth," it is because he wants to glorify Wisdom for his benefits and reveal the salvific history to the people of his era. If we seek Wisdom, let us remember, with Louis Marie, that "he allows himself to easily be seen to those who love him," but we will never be finished knowing him on this earth. His excellence is so miraculous that it is unutterable and cannot be grasped: "the Holy Spirit, having taken the pain to show us the excellence of Wisdom...in such sublime and intelligible terms, that we only have to report it here with a few reflections" (ASE 52). The message is clear. How can we not recognize the authority of this inspired text along with him? We can pray a prayer of praise, using the first few verses of the prologue to John (1:1–5).

The vigor of the Gospels inspires and spurs Louis Marie's spirituality. During his youth, he asked: "How do you expect me to remain quiet?" But the time came when he had matured. He "wanted to learn to speak well" so that the servant of God would be "fulfilled," and "equipped" for his apostolic work. In the same way as Paul, he knew that it would be up to him to teach, refute, straighten out, and correct, for the false wisdoms of the world would come into opposition with Wisdom. "God has his Wisdom; and he is the sole and true one which must be loved and sought like a great treasure. But those who have been corrupted by the world also have their wisdoms which must be condemned..." (ASE 74). In his era, Louis Marie had to confront the opposition of many of his contemporaries. Just like the prophet Ezekiel, who symbolically ate the book of the Word of Yahweh, he gained strength through

the Holy Spirit of God. We, also, can accept this recommendation: "O mortal, eat what is offered to you; eat this scroll, and
go, speak to the house of Israel" (Ezek 3:1). Let us pray to
Eternal Wisdom. May we learn to "speak well" so that we
may inspire others with his love.

> O divine Wisdom, sovereign of heaven and earth, hum-
> bly prostrated before you, I ask your forgiveness for
> being so bold as to speak of your greatness.... I beg
> you to not look upon the shadows of my spirit and the
> impurities of my mouth, or, if you do, may it be only
> to destroy them with a blink of your eye and a breath
> from your mouth. You have so much beauty and gentle-
> ness, you have protected me from so much evil and
> filled me with so many benefits, and yet you are still so
> unknown and misunderstood. How could I remain si-
> lent? Not only justice and knowledge, but my own in-
> terest obligates me to speak of you, even if I stutter.
> Like a child, I could only stutter, it is true, but it is
> because I am still a stuttering child that I want to learn
> how to speak well, so that when I reach the fullness of
> your age....
>   My admirable prince, recognize...in the stroke of
> my pen, just how many steps I have taken to find you;
> and give as many blessings and enlightenments to those
> whom I want to make aware of and speak of you, so
> that all who hear of you will be inflamed with a new
> desire to love you and possess you in time and for eter-
> nity (ASE 1–2).

REFLECTION QUESTIONS

Do I make a practice of reading the Bible? Do I attempt different methods of prayer in this practice? Might I consider *lectio divina* (that is, the practice of placing myself within a Gospel story—imagining I am there—and contemplating this experience in a silent and prayerful manner) as a part of my prayer life? Would discussing the incorporation of structured scriptural reading into my prayer life with a priest or spiritual director be helpful to me at this time?

To Jesus Through Mary

FOCUS POINT

"In order to find God's grace, we must find Mary." Mary is the first saint, the most perfect of all creatures. We must all strive to be as welcoming as the Mother of our Lord. It was her welcoming docility that made her so attractive to God, that invited his will to participate in her life at the Annunciation. May we all welcome the will of God into our lives with such openness, and may Mary, full of grace, bring our prayers to our heavenly Father and bring to us his graces so that our union with him may deepen.

Living image of God, bought with the precious blood of Jesus Christ, the will of God is with you and you will become holy just like him in this life, and glorious like him in the other. "Be perfect, therefore, as your heavenly Father is perfect" (Mt 5:48).

The acquisition of God's holiness is your vocation; it is to there that your thoughts, words, actions, suffering, and all the movements of your life must be aimed; or you resist God by not doing what you have been created to do.

O, what an admirable work! Dust changed into light...the creature in the Creator and a man in God! O admirable work! I repeat it, but it is a work that is difficult in itself and impossible for a single nature; there is only God, who, through a single grace, an abundant and extraordinary grace, can succeed....

What will you do? What means will you select to show where God calls you? The ways of salvation and holiness are known to all, written in the Gospels, explained by the spiritual masters, practiced by the saints, and necessary for all who want to save themselves and arrive at perfection. These means are: humbleness of heart, continuous prayer, universal mortification, self-abandonment to Divine Providence, and conformity to the will of God.

In order to practice all of these means of salvation and holiness, grace and God's help are absolutely necessary, and this grace is given to all...no one should doubt that....

Everything is reduced to finding an easy way to obtain the necessary grace from God to become holy; and that is what I want to learn. And, in order to get the necessary grace from God, I say that you must find Mary (SM 3–6).

L ouis Marie did not seek to write a book of devotion to the Blessed Virgin; and it is by penetrating us with his theological intuition that we can give a just meaning to his Marian teaching. To the base of his spiritual building is situated, like a cornerstone, the motto which he lived, shared with his companions, and willed to his descendants: "God alone." In 1715, he wrote the following to Marie-Louise Trichet (the first Daughter of Wisdom), to ask her to leave Poitiers to go to Rochelle; he used this occasion to guide her: "I know that you will have difficulties to conquer; but it is necessary for that enterprise which is so glorious to God and salvific to our neighbor to be sprinkled with thorns and crosses. And if we don't risk anything for God, we will do nothing great for him.... Everything for you, God alone" (L 27). A spiritual product of the French schools, Louis Marie, remarkably, had a sense of the grandeur of God and the glory that is due him: he is the All-Everything. Particularly in his youth, Louis Marie manifested a "singularly" sensory tenderness towards Mary, absolute confidence in her: "Everything pertaining to him had been done when he had prayed to his good Mother, and he no longer hesitated...." One, however, must not think that he elevated her higher that her status as a creature. He clearly explained it: "I ardently love Mary / after God my Savior"—"Jesus finds his glory / in the honor we give her. To place her first / To love her without imitating her / is a great error / that we cannot forgive" (C 76, 1–3). What Louis Marie wanted to confide to us was the secret for holiness. He wanted to transmit the knowledge and practice of a marvelous way for holiness that, he said, "the Most High taught him." It takes a knowledge of Mary and of the marvels of grace operated by God in her. Before discovering this truth, he invites us to pray to the Holy Spirit and Mary "to request the grace to understand and taste of the divine mystery" (see SM 1–2). We can pray the "Veni Creator" and the "Ave Maria Stella."

Louis Marie assures us that "the acquisition of God's holiness is our assured vocation," that we are created "as the liv-

ing image of God." God wanted to reserve a superior dignity
to man in creation, elevating him all the way to his resem-
blance in order to be able to abase himself to the level of
humanity to redeem them with the blood of Jesus Christ. Already saved, we are all called to unite with the multitude men-
tioned in the Book of Revelation. But, "Who are these, robed
in white, and where have they come from?" (7:13). They are
the men and women of earth, who progress, painfully at times,
with their God and with the love of their brothers. "These are
they who have come out of the great ordeal: they have washed
their robes and made them white in the blood of the Lamb"
(Rev 7:14). The saints did not go beyond their humanity. They
assumed it, anchored in the realities of their lives, trying to
fulfill it bountifully and by identifying themselves more closely
to Christ, the Eternal and Incarnate Wisdom. Thus, there is a
potential saint in each of us. Louis Marie tells us that it suf-
fices that all of the thoughts, words, actions, suffering, and
movements of our lives aim toward a loving response to the
desire of God. Called to become God: a project that is "admirable" but "difficult," if not "impossible," without grace. The
saint, who has experienced it personally, teaches us that "in
order to find God's grace, we must find Mary."

In order to be faithful to our vocation as baptized persons,
to "climb where God calls us," Louis Marie commits us to
pass through Mary, to contemplate Mary, God's first adorer
"in spirit and truth," the first one to ascend to sainthood.

She let the Holy Spirit work in her. Through her, "the Word
of God was made flesh," and Wisdom came to dwell "amongst
us." Let us take the time to meditate about Mary's attitude at
the Annunciation. We can ask her to transfer her perfect docility to the Spirit to us, to help us become aware of our resis-
tance to the actions of the Holy Spirit within us. Let us allow

ourselves to be transformed by the Holy Spirit under the gaze of Mary. Think of Mary so that Mary, in our place, can think of God. "When we praise her, love her, honor her, or give to her, God is honored, we give to God through Mary and in Mary" (VD 225).

The call to become holy, because God is holy and he wants to make us share his glory, is welcomed with joy by all people of good will. However, we do lose our trust at times; our weakness, inconsistency, and vulnerabilities invade our spirit and heart. Louis Marie tells us: "There is no place where the creature could find God closer to it and more proportioned to its weakness than in Mary, it is then for this reason that he came to earth" (SM 20). Therefore, let us shape ourselves in the image of Jesus Christ, relying upon nothing of our own, "throwing ourselves into Mary, letting ourselves be molded through the operation of the Holy Spirit there" (see SM 18). He will make us understand the manner in which Wisdom approaches man: "He only had to say this single word to Mary Magdalene: Mary, and she was filled with joy and gentleness" (ASE 122). God's holiness, the imprint of tenderness and mercy, removes the veil that conceals sin, holds our hand, and lifts up the sinner. With Louis Marie, let us ask Mary to accompany us all along our road of holiness, and to remember that holiness is a work that takes a lifetime. May she help us advance to and reach our destination with perseverance, to become holy through the grace of God. "When you follow her, you do not take a wrong turn; when you pray to her, you do not lose hope; when she dwells in your thoughts, you are sheltered from errors; when she supports you, you don't fall; when she protects you, you have no fears, when she leads you, you never tire; when she is favorable to you, you reach salvation" (SM 40).

Louis Marie gives Mary a privileged place in God's plan. He parallels her role in the Incarnation, "filled with grace" by the Trinity which is transferred to her for giving Jesus to the world; and her role in the prolongation of the Incarnation, where the salvation of humanity through the sanctification of the members of the Body of Christ is realized in the Church. Through our confirmation, we are all responsible for the mission of the Church. Let us not forget that Mary had been chosen by God to carry and give birth to the infant Jesus. Louis Marie told us that: "All of the grace and all of God's gifts pass through her hands" (SM 10). Therefore, it is through Mary that we can lead our friends to Jesus. We can ask her to make us true disciples of Wisdom, able to fulfill the "new" visitations, bearers of grace for the hearts who seek God. "…(May) all of us come to the unity of the faith and of the knowledge of the Son of God, to maturity, to the measure of the full stature of Christ" (Eph 4:13).

> Here, my dear Mistress, this is what good I have done through the grace of your dear Son; I am not able to keep it because of my weakness and inconsistency…. Alas, if we see, every day, the cedars of Lebanon fall into the mud, and the eagles, lifting themselves up to the sun, become birds of the night; a thousand just fall to my left and ten thousand to my right, but…my most powerful Princess, keep all of my good work…hold me up so that I do not fall; I entrust you…with all that I have. I know who you are, that is why I entrust myself completely to you; you are faithful to God and to man, and you do not permit anything entrusted to you to perish; you are powerful, nothing can hurt you, nor harm what you have in your care (SM 40).

REFLECTION QUESTIONS

How do I attempt to emulate the welcoming docility of Mary in my own life? Do I bristle when I am faced with challenges and growth obstacles in my daily life? Or do I embrace these challenges, and open myself to the grace of growth and deepening union with God that these experiences will reward me? How can I maintain this openness in all of my encounters with the people of God? Might a daily rosary help me in these efforts to keep a Marian welcoming alive in my heart?

DAY EIGHT

The Irrevocable Gift of Our Heart

FOCUS POINT

We are servants—no, slaves—of our Lord. He is our creator and we are his creatures, and we must recognize this reality in our humility. We are created to serve God in all that we think, do, and say. There is no other purpose to our lives than to serve God; anything less, and we are untrue to our calling as creatures created in his image. Jesus is our model in this service. He is the perfect man, the one who gave back to the Father everything he received. We are called to do the same.

I say that we must be for Jesus Christ and serve him, not only as mercenary servants, but like loving slaves who, under the effect of great love, give ourselves to serve him...solely for the honor it brings him (VD 73).

Baptism has made us true slaves of Jesus Christ...the unique source...and the sole end of all our good works... (VD 68).

Let us make an irrevocable gift of our heart to the Eternal and Incarnate Wisdom of God, which is all that is asked of us (ASE 132).

M odern sensitivity bristles and is revolted when it hears the words "slave" and "slavery," and rightfully so. How can we act otherwise when faced with people who are exploited or reduced by their neighbor to dehumanizing servitude? How can we not disapprove of and condemn servitude of all types?

Louis Marie knew that the word "slave" could be badly interpreted. Thus, he took the trouble to explain himself at length (VD 68–73) without either diminishing or denying reality: baptized persons must be conscious of their total "belonging" to Jesus. He insists upon the situation that is radically new to the baptized person: "We do not, in any way, belong to ourselves, as the Apostle said (see 1 Cor 6:19; 12:27), but completely to him as his members and the slaves he has purchased...paying the price with his blood" (VD 68). The term "servant" appeared too weak to him; the servant didn't give all that he was, nor all that he possessed, he could ask for wages for his services, and he could work for his master for just a limited time (see VD 71): in modern terms—an employee. However, through baptism, we freely consent to give ourselves entirely to Christ and to serve him without profit or gaining any advantage for ourselves. We deliver ourselves without reservation and for all time, we fulfill the irrevocable gift of ourselves to God.

Jesus Christ was the first to take on "the condition of a

slave" (the ecumenical translation of the Bible says "servant," but a footnote in Phil 2:7 states "rather, a slave"). He did that in order to reveal the trinitarian love for us and invite us to be a part of it, in order to save us from sin and convey his life as the Son to us. In and through him, we are all children of God.

"Blessed be the God and Father of our Lord Jesus Christ, who has blessed us in Christ with every spiritual blessing in the heavenly places, just as he chose us in Christ before the foundation of the world to be holy and blameless before him in love. He destined us for adoption as his children through Jesus Christ, according to the good pleasure of his will" (Eph 1:3–5)

Yes, Father, may you be blessed! Long before you created our world and the cosmos, you thought about man, about each person you would call to existence when the time would come.

You thought about me and already loved me. You thought about all of my brothers and sisters and loved each of them. Immensely, without measuring in your Father's heart, revealed through your Son, "the firstborn within a large family" (Rom 8:29) "who loved me and gave himself for me" (Gal 2:20). Help me to marvel like Saint John: "See what love the Father has given us, that we should be called children of God; and that is what we are. The reason the world does not know us is that it did not know him. Beloved, we are God's children now..." (1 Jn 3:1–2).

The Psalmist wrote: "What are human beings that you are mindful of them...yet you have made them a little lower than God..." (Ps 8:4–5). After having made us "in your image" (see Gen 1:27), you are simply in the process of "edifying" us: "what we will be has not yet been revealed. What we do know is this: when he is revealed, we will be like him..." (1 Jn 3:2). Astonishing, yes! But the astonishment is that we do not astonish ourselves.

I am baptized: the grace of the sacrament remains active at each moment in as much as I give my consent to it. "God's love has been poured into our hearts through the Holy Spirit and has been given to us" (Rom 5:5). The goal of the baptismal life is that the presence of the Holy Spirit in me would be so incorporated into my being that it, little by little, changes my thoughts, words, love, and behavior into that of Christ. "It is no longer I who live, but it is Christ who lives in me" (Gal 2:20).

I have a sort of "dual citizenship," that of heaven and that of the earth. A new life, of a radical newness, unheard of, a new identity introduced into my being through baptism: I have been anointed just like Jesus. In that way, I have become a member of Christ, God's Anointed One "par excellence" (above all others), the one who receives everything from the Father, belongs totally to him and gives him everything he is: "you belong to Christ, and Christ belongs to God" (1 Cor 3:23). Louis Marie gave priority to his Christian identity. Through his biological father, he was Grignion; through the place of his baptism, he was "de Montfort," or simply, "Montfort," and that is how he signed many of his letters, even one, in 1704, to his own mother, speaking of the "new family" to which he belonged (see L 20). Incorporated into the Church, a part of the people of the Covenant, he could say to the Holy Spirit: "You alone have baptized me, at my baptism, I have married you" (see C 27, 11; C 98, 13, 16, 21).

During his parish missions, he reminded Christians of the fundamental importance of their baptism and he made them renew the "wishes" or "promises." He proposed this renewal like an orientation for their life, the consequence of a real conversion, a true "contract of a covenant," solemnly written and signed. It was this which Pope Clement XI had asked of him and what he prescribed for the missionaries who joined him: he aimed to renew the spirit of Christianity within Christians. He sought to make each baptized person aware of their total dependence on Christ, in which baptism places them and through love, to give their consent.

To be baptized is something special, as Saint Paul tells us: "Now...you are...members of the household of God" (Eph 2:19). "Lead a life worthy of the calling to which you have been called...live in love...live as children of light...be careful then how you live, not as unwise people..." (Eph 4:1; 5:2, 8, 15).

"Live in love" (Eph 5:2) sums up the new way to live as a Christian. It is to love God and to love man, just as they are, with the love of God received at baptism. It is also to welcome the gift of love so that we become a gift ourselves, all given to God through adoration, praise, faithfulness to the Word, all given to others through concrete attention, sharing, service, respect, and forgiveness.

That is the Christian life, filial and fraternal. That is my life as a baptized Christian.

It is still true that I remain weak, fragile, and a sinner. My total belonging to Jesus Christ—or my "loving enslavement"— is often not very conscious, poorly assured, or practically denounced. With Louis Marie, I could only repeat:

O Incarnate Wisdom! O most lovable and adorable Jesus, true God and true man, only Son of the eternal Father and of Mary, ever virgin!

I thank you for what you have negated in yourself, by taking on the form of a slave.... But alas! Unfaithful and ungrateful that I am, I have not kept the promises I have solemnly made at my baptism to you: I have, in no way, fulfilled my obligations; I do not deserve to be called your child, nor your slave.... On my own, I don't dare approach your...majesty. That is why I have recourse to the intercession and mercy of your most holy Mother, whom you have given to me as a mediator next to you; it is in that way that I hope to obtain contrition and forgiveness from you for my sins, the acquisition and conservation of Wisdom.

O Mary...I am an unfaithful sinner. Today, I renew and confirm, in your hands, my baptismal wishes; I repudiate the devil forever...and I give myself completely to Jesus Christ, Wisdom Incarnate, in order to carry my cross as he did, all the days of my life, so that I will be more faithful to him than I have been up until now.... Amen (ASE 223–225).

REFLECTION QUESTIONS

In what ways do I practice humility in my life? Do I place myself at the service of others, below even those that the world would tell me are not worth my attention? Do I place my own needs aside when I am faced with the needs of the poor and hungry? How do I respond in the face of such need? Might I forego a meal to unite myself in some way with the greater need that exists in the poorer areas of the world? Might I put that money or food I have denied myself into a local food pantry or charity?

To Give Everything to Mary, to Lose Oneself in Her

FOCUS POINT

Mary is our great intercessor. During the wedding at Cana, it was Mary who interceded on behalf of the newly married couple so as to help them avoid embarrassment by running out of wine during their wedding celebration. As Mary asked Jesus to help at the wedding, so she asks for God's graces to be given to us when we ask for divine aid in our own lives. Mary was the first to carry the Lord inside her; her tie to the Lord is great, and he will deny her nothing she asks of him.

All of our perfection consists in conforming, uniting, and consecrating ourselves to Jesus Christ. The most perfect of all devotions is without difficulty when we conform, unite, and consecrate ourselves the most perfectly to Jesus Christ. Mary was the most conformed to Jesus Christ...it follows that the more a soul is consecrated to Mary, the more it will be to Jesus Christ.

That is why perfect consecration to Jesus Christ is nothing other than a perfect and complete consecration of oneself to the Most Blessed Virgin, which is the devotion I teach; otherwise explained, a perfect renewal of the wishes and promises of holy baptism.

Therefore, this devotion consists of giving oneself completely to the Most Blessed Virgin in order to completely belong to Jesus Christ, through her....

O, how happy is the man who gives everything to Mary, entrusts and loses himself in and of everything in Mary! He is all to Mary and she is everything to him (see VD 120, 121, 179).

In his book, *True Devotion to the Blessed Virgin*, Louis Marie put into words what he had been teaching for many years in his missions, as well as personally living on a daily basis. Therefore, he has given us what he has lived, his intimate and mystical experience.

His "loving enslavement" to Jesus Christ, the consequence of baptism, is nothing other than a gift, given without reservations, of himself to Mary, which led him, by degrees, under the action of the Holy Spirit to a transformation in Jesus Christ (see VD 119).

By acting in this manner, he imitated the very conduct of God himself, he took the same road that the Holy Trinity followed: "The Father only gave and only gives his Son through her, only makes children for himself through her, only transfers his graces through her; God the Son had only been formed...through her, is only formed each day and engendered through her in the union with the Holy Spirit, and only transfers his merits and virtues through her; the Holy Spirit only formed Jesus Christ through her, only forms the members of his Mystical Body through her, only dispenses his gifts and favors through her. After such pressing examples as these of the very Holy Trinity, how could we, without severe blindness, pass over Mary, not consecrate ourselves to her and depend upon her to go to God in order to sacrifice ourselves to God?" (VD 140). "Saint Bernard said, is it not just that grace returns to its author by the same pathway by which it has come to us?" (SM 35).

In our progression towards God, Mary, far from being an obstacle, constitutes, through the will of God, a compelling passage. A woman does not give birth to the Head without its members, but to the entire Body. Christians, since they are members of the Body of Christ, have the same Mother as Jesus: "Woman, here is your son...here is your mother" (Jn 19:26–27).

When we give ourselves totally to Mary, we accept her as our Mother in order to receive from God, through her, the life as "adoptive children"; it is to make the gift from God become "effective" by welcoming it; therefore glorifying God in the most sure manner: "You never praise nor honor Mary without her praising and honoring God with you. Mary is connected to God, and I would do well to call her...God's echo who only says and repeats what God does. If you call on Mary, she calls on God" (VD 225). It is, once again, to use the same pathway of spiritual infancy, filial trust and interior freedom, "a road that is simple, short, perfect, and sure in order to reach the union with Jesus Christ" (VD 152). In Mary, "the saints are formed and molded" (VD 118). "The person who is thrown into this spiritual mold is quickly formed and molded into Jesus Christ and he in him: at virtually no cost and in a short time, he becomes a God since he was thrown into the same mold in which God was formed" (VD 219). This path is not egoistic, it even allows one to express the highest point of love towards his neighbor since Mary could dispose of us as she wishes in service to her other children, our brothers and sisters (see SM 39, VD 171, 172).

How could we refuse such a pathway? Louis Marie wrote: "I would rather die than live without being everything to Mary." But he knew, through experience, of his fragility and the necessity to be constantly starting again. "Thousands of times, I was there at the foot of the cross with John the Evangelist and just as many times, I gave myself to her; but I have not yet done it according to your wishes, my dear Jesus, I do it now just like you...will me to do this; and if you see something in my soul and body that doesn't belong to this majestic Princess, I beg for you to remove it and throw it far away from me, for, not belonging to Mary, it is unworthy of you" (SM 66).

In order to accept Mary into oneself, it is necessary to give her all the space, and to do that one must void oneself of one's self-love, strip oneself of one's "old self" in order to identify oneself with the "me" of Jesus Christ, the son of Mary. "What is essential for this devotion consists in the interior that she will form" (VD 119, 226), an interior of the disciple of Jesus called to deny himself (see Mt 16:24), and to agree to "sacrifices for God" (VD 118). Louis Marie invites us to a humbleness, radical poverty, participation in an "emptying" (see Phil 2:7). To agree to this is a great gift from God.

Mary did not remain inactive. Taking her mission and maternal role seriously, she intercedes with her son. For those who ask, she obtains what they need. Particularly, the gift of faith: a pure faith, a faith that is vivid and driven by charity, a faith that is unmovable as a rock, a faith that is in action and courageous. She frees the heart of all misgivings and fears; she opens it to the freedom that is the love that belongs to the children of God. She fills the soul with confidence and transfers her own spirit into it. By giving ourselves totally to Mary, by "losing ourselves...to the abyss of her interior," we rapidly become "living copies of Mary, to love and glorify Jesus Christ"; to Mary we offer the possibility of carrying "the fruit of her era, and this fruit is none other than Jesus Christ" (see VD 214–218).

"When will the souls breathe in Mary as much as they breathe in the air?" (VD 217). It is up to each of us to take the necessary steps: to be driven by a strong desire, with confidence and perseverance, to ask for the courage necessary to let Mary work in us as she wishes, in order to become "the natural portrait of Jesus Christ" (VD 220). The only condition is to truly accept to lose everything, to lose oneself in Mary. Then, we live in Mary, as in a divine milieu and she is at home within us. "Here is only what we can believe / I carry her in the middle of myself / Engraved with traits of glory / Even through the obscurity of faith...I do everything in and through her / That is the secret for holiness / To always be faithful to God / To always do his will in all things" (C 77, 15 and 19).

To do everything through Mary is to renounce one's own spirit in order to deliver oneself to hers, then dwell in her hands "like a tool in the hands of a workman, like a lute in the hands of a musician...to lose oneself and abandon oneself in her like a stone we throw into the sea," renewed from time to time, during and after the action, the gift of oneself, by saying, for example: "I renounce myself, I give myself to my dear Mother" (VD 259). Such an attitude, renewed day after day, leads us to imitate Mary, just as a child imitates its Mother.

"How happy a soul is when...it is all possessed and governed by Mary's spirit, which is a spirit that is both gentle and strong, zealous and prudent, humble and brave, pure and fruitful!" (VD 258). It can't keep this secret for holiness to itself. It seeks to transfer it to make Mary known and loved: "We must draw the whole world, if we can, to serve her and to this true and solid devotion.... In this way, a good servant and slave must not remain inactive; he must, supported by her protection, undertake to do great things for this majestic Sovereign, to do everything for her, with the only reward being the honor to belong to such an admirable Princess and the happiness to be united to Jesus, her son, through her with a connection that is indissoluble, for now and all eternity" (see VD 265).

All of it sums up to "perform one's actions through Mary, with Mary, in Mary, and for Mary, so that they are perfectly done through Jesus, with Jesus, in Jesus, and for Jesus " (VD 257).

In as much as we constantly and increasingly renew our confidence and loving dependence we show her, Mary works in us "as it appears good to the greater glory of her son and through her son, Jesus, for the glory of the Father."

Hail Mary, very lovable daughter of the eternal Father, admirable Mother of the Son, very faithful Spouse of the Holy Spirit, majestic Temple of the most Holy Trinity. Hail sovereign Princess, to whom everything is submitted in heaven and on earth. Hail assured Refuge of sinners, Our Lady of Mercy who has never refused anyone. Sinner that I am, I throw myself at your feet, and I beg for you to obtain for me...from your dear son, with divine Wisdom, contrition and forgiveness for all my sins. I consecrate myself completely to you with all that I am. Today, I take you for my Mother and my Mistress; treat me as the last of your children, and the most submissive of your servants...so that it not be said to all who have recourse to you, that I have been the first to have been abandoned! O my hope! O my life! O my faithful and Immaculate Virgin Mary! Answer me, defend me, nourish me, teach me, save me. Amen (MR 15).

REFLECTION QUESTIONS

Do I, like Mary, seek to clear a space in my own life so that God may take his rightful place inside me? Do I call upon Mary's assistance when I am in need? Do I attempt to shape my obedience to God according to the model given by the Blessed Virgin? Do I accept Mary as my guide in faith? Do I seek to build my faith life in the manner she lived, with the spiritual abandonment she lived so that the Lord might fill me with his grace and divine will?

DAY TEN

I Thank God
a Thousand Times
for Passing As a Poor Person

FOCUS POINT

When we pass as a poor person in this life (that is, as a humble person, poor in spirit, open to God's love and the love of others, not relying on ourselves), we shine like a beacon of love. We tell the world, "I am receptive to everyone's love and to the goodness of God. Come to me." Inevitably, we are approached by both God and neighbor, and we are never left wanting. This poverty of spirit unites us with those who are truly poor (materially) and truly broken (spiritually). From this state of being, we can begin to heal with God's love.

To Mr. Leschassier, Superior of the seminary of Saint Sulpice. Poitiers, May 4, 1701.

...I arrived at Poitiers...and I was forced to wait for the Monsignor of Poitiers for four days....

During this time, I made a short retreat in a small room in which I was enclosed in the middle of a great city, where I knew no one. I took it upon myself, however, to go to the hospital to minister to the corporal needs of the poor there, if I could not to their spiritual ones. I went to pray (to God) in their little church, where I spent around four hours awaiting supper, which appeared to be a very short time. It appeared, however, quite long to a few poor people who, having seen me on my knees, with a habit that was so like theirs, went to tell others and who, excitedly entered, one after another, pushing forward to give me alms; some gave more, others less. All of this happened without my knowledge. I finally left the church to ask when we would have supper and, at the same time, for permission to set the table for the poor; but, on the one hand, I was much mistaken, having learned that they don't eat in the community, and very surprised on the other, having learned that they wanted to give me alms and had given the order to the porter to not let me leave. I thank God a thousand times for passing as a poor person and bringing these glorious benefits, and I thank my dear brothers and sisters for their good will.

Since that time, they have shown me such affection to publicly say that I am their priest... (L 6).

Louis Marie spent his adolescence in the proximity of and caring for the little ones and the humble for whom he had an attraction, tenderness, and veneration. At the end of his studies, he carried a life's project within him: to follow Christ, having selected radical evangelism. His ardent desire for the priesthood was to be realized, and he left Rennes to go to the Saint Sulpice Seminary in Paris. He left with an attitude of total abandonment into the arms of Divine Providence, symbolizing "his passage with the poor." Leaving the house, he left on foot like a vagabond, his friends accompanying as far as the Cesson Bridge, a few leagues from Rennes. That is where the definitive rupture came with his social identity. It became concrete through a gesture that was very significant: at the side of the road, a beggar spoke to him…he gave him the money his father had given him for the journey. Then, he stripped off his new habit that his mother had made and traded it with the beggar for the rags he was wearing. These would become his new clothes!

In order to be like the poor, Louis Marie made the effort to approach the poor brother in whom he saw Jesus Christ. He was not satisfied to serve the underprivileged, he concretely united with the downtrodden and marginalized people. He learned their culture and let it enter his heart so well that he became known as one of them. He understood that spiritual help passed through attention to a humanity. It was the intensity of his prayer, but also the tenderness of his gaze, the fraternal gesture of his compassion, that earned him "election" as "their" priest. All of this was not improvised. It was the fruit of a profound interior life, of a contemplation of Christ in his Incarnation. He was overcome with divine Wisdom who made himself a poor person by assuming the human condition, and he wanted to reproduce this poverty in his life. "For you know the generous act of our Lord Jesus Christ, that though he was rich, yet for your sakes he became poor, so that by his poverty you might become rich" (2 Cor 8:9). Witnesses of many forms of poverty in our society, don't we run the risk of taking satisfaction in humanitarian activism? We could take the path that Louis Marie shows us. To what source will it lead us? To what detachment will it provoke us? The example he set with his life could help us to put everything into question, for it was a true kind of poverty.

In fact, if Louis Marie lived an effective material kind of poverty, beyond that, he had endured it to the extreme of both a moral and psychological stripping. Very soon after his ordination, he found himself poor and humbled in his most legitimate spiritual aspirations, deprived of friends, reputation, recognition, and understanding. He was a man who was broken in his youth, and that would last five years. The following well illustrates this situation: at the end of several months of tireless devotion at the Salpêtrière in Paris, "one evening, he found his dismissal papers under his plate." He took refuge in a hovel under a stairway. It is from there, it seems, that he wrote to Marie-Louise Trichet, who would be the first religious sister in the congregation he would found: "I feel that you continue, for this poor, sickly sinner, to ask God for divine Wisdom, through the means of crosses, humiliations, poverty.... I feel the effect of your prayers, for, more than ever, I am even more impoverished, crucified, humiliated..." (L 6).

To our way of thinking, a poor person is most often perceived as someone who is lacking the necessities of life, no matter what the nature of his needs. For Louis Marie, the title "poor person" represented a type of supreme recognition: he, the one who was so happy to have passed for being a poor person! With a glance of faith, he transformed their humble reality: "They are true portraits of Jesus Christ who was poor for us, they are his identical brothers, worthy to be honored by all" (C 20, 17). He gave such value to the poor person, "it is because, for him, they were like a sacrament that contained Jesus Christ hidden under their unapproachable exterior," a tangible sign of his presence among us, a means of access to the mystery of God which had clothed itself in human weakness. He said: "a poor person is a great mystery; we must know how to solve it." His conviction pushed him to love and serve them as if they were lords and masters, at times, to excess!

To pray with Louis Marie is to unite oneself with his search for Wisdom. There, our gaze will see beyond indifference and our compassion will take the shape of effective service. God, Father of the poor, give us the divine Wisdom that comes from you.

Louis Marie was a great missionary in the Church of the seventeenth century. In that era, the spiritualists, seized and marveled by the glory of God, judged that man belonged to God and was there for him. That carried with it two attitudes: adoration and service. Conscious of the precarious state of society, Louis Marie's apostolic spirituality would orient itself towards the poor and blossom in favor of the poor. It was to the honor of God that the poor were recognized, respected, and taken into consideration, so that they would get out of the state of poverty. In this way, Louis Marie, faithful to his attractions and the needs of the time, committed himself to the cause of the poor. With as much boldness as talent, he waged a courageous war with a view to increase the rights of the poor and alleviate their living conditions. For example: at the general hospital in Poitiers, he introduced reforms, not without opposition, with respect to their practices and regulations, to the benefit of the poor "inmates." His confidence in man made him discover the living vigor of the beatitudes in the poor, and he gave thanks to the Father to have hidden "things" from the wise and intelligent, and having revealed them to the little ones and the humble (see Mt 11:25–26). At Louis Marie's invitation, we can commit ourselves to a fight against poverty and reach out to those in distress. We can also ask ourselves about what recognition we give to the poor and how we can make their plight reach our hearts. May the Poor One reach our hearts and inspire our prayers.

Let us contemplate Incarnate Wisdom with Louis Marie who, still today, through his Christian intermediaries, wants to get closer to the poor, the little ones, and the sinners. "Wisdom is tender and gentle towards man, and particularly towards the poor sinners..." (ASE 126). Let us stand up to the challenge through our conduct and attitudes.

> The poor and the little children followed him everywhere, they saw him as one of them; in this dear Savior, they saw such simplicity, kindness, condescension, and charity, they pressed closer to him.... The poor saw him dressed poorly and simply in every way, without ostentation or pride, nothing pleased them more than being with him; as for him, from his perspective, he gave them a thousand praises and blessings whenever he met them...with such gentleness, he treated Mary Magdalene the sinner, with such gentle condescension, he converted the Samaritan, with such mercy he forgave the adulterous woman... (ASE 124–125).

REFLECTION QUESTIONS

How do I approach the poor in my world? Do I simply throw money in their direction and walk away? Or do I evaluate what it means to be poor, what it means to want in a spiritual and material way? Do I unite myself in need with the poor and broken through fasting, through self-denial? How does this openness to poverty aid me in loving those who are poor materially and broken spiritually? Does it not make me more "in tune" with the needs of these people and does it not provide a channel of grace by which these people can feel my love and God's love through me?

DAY ELEVEN

The Loving Invention of the Eucharist

FOCUS POINT

"Wisdom made himself become nourishment." So that he could continue to nourish us and provide for us after he left his earthly life, Jesus fulfilled his promise to be with us always by the loving intention of the Eucharist. Loving us so much and seeking an intimate union wit his creation, Jesus comes us to us in the bread of Communion, feeding our spiritual hunger, providing for us in our need, and touching the most intimate parts of our being. In the Blessed Sacrament, Wisdom has become nourishment, and all of creation is fulfilled.

Eternal Wisdom, in order to get close to man and give tangible witness to his love, went so far as to become a man, become a child, become poor, and die for us all on the cross....

On the one hand, wanting to show his love for man all the way to dying in his place in order to save him, unable to resolve to do anything except leave man, Wisdom found an admirable secret in order to live and die at the same time, and dwell with man until the end of time: it was the loving invention of the Eucharist; and to get the result of satisfying his love in this mystery, he had no difficulty in changing and reversing all nature.

If Wisdom doesn't hide in the striking beauty of a diamond or other precious stone, it is because he doesn't want to just live with man; but he hides himself under the guise of a small piece of bread, which is man's own nourishment, so that, having been eaten by man, he goes into him all the way to his heart so as to take his pleasures there....

A saint said: "O eternal Wisdom, O God, truly a prodigy of himself through the desire he has for man...."

If we are not touched by fervent desires, loving searches, and testimonies of the love of this lovable Wisdom, how hard and ungrateful must we be?....

Let us then desire and only seek divine Wisdom..."for wisdom is better than jewels and all that you may desire cannot compare with her" (Prov 8:11): we can desire nothing more than Wisdom. Thus, if you desire a few gifts from God or a few heavenly treasures, and you do not desire Wisdom, you desire something less (ASE 70–73).

———

The testimonies of his friend, Mr. Blain, give us a foreshadowing of the ascent of the eucharistic mystery on Louis Marie's spirituality and fervor. In the community in Paris: "Louis Marie took Communion four times a week, but he gave it such devotion that it was something to see. No matter that his entire life was a spiritual preparation for this holy action, he added special dispositions to it on the night before.... His thanksgiving lasted an hour, and, in order to do it with more quietness and to rejoice in the presence of his beloved, he looked for places in the church that were more hidden." On a pilgrimage to Chartres: "Louis Marie took Communion with such a fervor and piety that the grace of God seemed to be at its apex, and he stayed there for six or eight hours straight...on his knees, immobile and enraptured." His attitude was in perfect harmony with his words: "I am outside of myself / by seeing the abasement / Where the Supreme Grandeur / Is in the Blessed Sacrament" (C 128, 1).

Louis Marie's burning attachment to the Blessed Sacrament is remarkable. It is the response of a saint to divine Love. It is of the order of grace, of a particular favor that comes from above and which gives access to and a taste for the mystery. Faced with this example, we question what place we give in our lives to the Eucharist; what understanding do we have of this spiritual reality, and what significance do we give to this gracious gift from God. All we have to do is grasp the humility of God, who could have overpowered us with his strength, but who chose to beg us for our love, in a whisper, hidden in a small piece of bread. We must grasp the eternal will of God, whose face shone on the face of Christ, and who chose to go beyond death, to remain present in the history of mankind until the end of all time. "A little while, and you will no longer see me, and again a little while, and you will see me" (Jn 16:16). Through these words, John made quite a distinction between the period that led to Jesus' death, and a new period granted to the disciples starting with the Resurrection. It was the time for the Church, and this time concerns all Christians.

We are all called to deepen our knowledge of the mode of
the presence of the glorified Christ in the world, and to live of
it. Through his spiritual experience, Louis Marie was well ahead
in the eucharistic mystery. Let us ask to be "the Body of Christ"
with him in the Church, to reflect the face of Incarnate Wisdom, today, to those who don't know about him, to become
the "broken bread" for a renewed fraternity.

Louis Marie, during his years at the seminary, took notes
about what particularly struck him in his courses. These un-
published notes give us an idea of what he was taught about
the Eucharist. By describing it as "an invention of love," he
used an expression that was dear to Mr. Olier, a great spiritual
master, whom he, unfortunately, did not know, but about whom
he heard a great deal spoken at Saint Sulpice, and whose teachings left their mark on him. In his book, *The Love of Eternal
Wisdom*, Louis Marie presented, in the same loving movement,
the three components for the salvation of man: the Incarnation, the Death, and the Eucharist. In his book, he wrote about
a God who was impassioned about the future of man. The
Incarnate and Crucified Wisdom of God bypassed the obstacle
of death by making himself become the Eucharist, by shaking
up nature in order to continue the route with his beloved humanity. Through his holiness and presence to the world, Louis
Marie revealed the invention of the love of Wisdom to those
he met. Wisdom also awaits our own participation. We can
ask for the grace of recognition for the gift of the Eucharist
that makes us a reflection of God for our brothers and sisters.

Louis Marie draws our attention to the way Wisdom chose
to establish his dwelling amongst us, just as he had promised
to the disciples after the Resurrection: "And remember, I am
with you always, to the end of the age" (Mt 28:20). Wisdom
did not seek to situate itself in the middle of the cosmos under

the guise of a flashy appearance. Instead, "Wisdom made himself become nourishment." Descending even lower, he wanted to be "eaten" to give a form, in an intimate union, to his loving desire to edify man. He wanted to have access to man's heart and "take his pleasures there." This attitude of poverty, which awaits everything from the other, is disturbing if we take the time to contemplate it. We know the experience of a happy relationship when we feel at ease with the person we meet. Wisdom wants to put us at ease, so he presents himself in a form that is familiar to us. Let us allow ourselves to be touched by the delight of love; by the trouble he went to in order to join us where we are; through this invitation to a response to divine Love. Louis Marie told us: "If we knew this infinite treasure Wisdom made for man, we would sigh both day and night to him." In order to know him, we must seek him. Let us be reminded that it is from the side of what is humble, without flash…. Let us ask him to help us turn to the poor.

The eucharistic marvel of the great missionary, filled as much with divine Wisdom as he wanted to be, wanted to share it. He was manifested with an ardent zeal to introduce the life of faith to the faithful through the missions. Louis Marie made them see Communion as an incomparable experience for the Christian. He had the conviction that the Eucharist was the instant, above all others, of transformation into Jesus Christ, and he judged that it must be preceded by a renewal of the promises of baptism and confession. For him, to receive Communion presupposed a serious commitment to conversion. "God gives his flesh to eat…so that we change into him" (C 132).

Along with Louis Marie, who teaches us always to use the intercession of the Blessed Virgin in order to speak to God, to get closer to him, and to unite with him, let us pray to divine Wisdom who has become the "Eucharist" (see VD 143).

I desire from you, O bread of life,
from today onward, without waiting for tomorrow.
I want to eat of you, I am dying of want.
I have a great hunger, give me some bread.
I am a blind person who cries out,
Lord Jesus, have pity on me!
Son of David, son of Mary,
whom I see, increase my faith.
I am incurably ill,
but with a single word you could cure me.
Without you, charitable doctor, it's all done,
I am going to die.
Lord, I knock at your door; my need is great,
I am dying of poverty.
I say in a tender and strong voice:
give me some charity.
Lord, I am,
I am unworthy to approach Communion.
Say a word, I will be worthy of it,
and come into my home (C 112, 4 and 7–10).

REFLECTION QUESTIONS

Do I recognize the nourishment and spiritual transformation when I receive the Eucharist? Does the "total giving" that is Jesus Christ make itself manifest in my daily life? Am I moved to give myself to the needs of others as God's instrument of love? Does the nourishment of the Eucharist assist me in seeing with new eyes—with eyes of love, the eyes of God—those people who I formerly found disagreeable and displeasing in a new light?

DAY TWELVE

To Make Our Lord Loved

FOCUS POINT

Like Louis de Montfort in his day, we are all commissioned by God to "make the Church." We all must imitate Wisdom (Jesus) if the world is to be transformed. It is by the passion of the Gospel, our passion for the Gospel, that the people who do not know God will come to know him by our love. There is a new evangelization on the horizon. It is an evangelization by the people of God for the people of God—all will come to the love the Lord by the love the Lord shows the world through us.

To Mr. Leschassier, Superior of the seminary of Saint Sulpice, Paris. Nantes, December 6, 1700.

In spite of myself, I did not find what I expected here, as holy a house as the Saint Sulpice Seminary, and that is why I left. Just as you, I had expected to go and get training with the missionaries, and, particularly, to share the catechism with the poor people, which is what attracted me. But I did nothing of that, and I don't even know if I will do it here, for there are so few subjects and no one has any experience except Mr. Lévêsque, but who, because of his advanced age, is not able to do any missions.... That being the case, I find, since I have been here, that I have been of two minds which seem opposed to each other. On the one hand, I feel a secret love for retreats and the hidden life...and on the other, I feel a great desire to make our Lord and his holy Mother loved, to go, in a poor and simple way, and give the catechism to the poor in the country, and to entice the sinners to the devotion to the Blessed Virgin.

That is what a good priest, who recently passed away was doing. He went from parish to parish to give the catechism to the peasants, depending solely on Divine Providence.... In the meantime, I work, even with some concern, to calm these desires, although they are good and continuous.... Just like in Paris, the desire comes to me...to go to Rennes and seek seclusion in a general hospital...there, to practice performing works of charity with the poor. But, I push away all of these desires...awaiting your advice, whether it is to remain here, for which I have no inclination, or to go elsewhere (L 5).

R ight from his youth, Louis Marie's life was completely oriented towards the coming of the reign of Jesus Christ into the world. A few words from Jean Baptiste Blain give witness to this: "Once his philosophy course was done, he no longer gave any thought to studying theology in depth in order to put himself in a position to fill the functions of an apostolic life to which he was destined." His vocation had its roots between two things he loved which mutually called to him: the love of Eternal Wisdom and love for the poor. It would be fulfilled between the two goals: to keep the spirit of the first apostles by truly following in Jesus' footsteps, and preparing for the coming of the kingdom in the perspective of "the end times." To pray with Louis Marie is to ask to live his faithfulness to an evangelical radicalism and to have his sharp conscience for the necessity to "make the Church."

In his book, *The Love of Eternal Wisdom*, he makes us go all the way to the source of his interior strength to the place where he draws his missionary dynamism. He attributes his spirituality and action to a pure and complete adhesion to the movements of trinitarian love, which reveal the intensity of his love for man through his incarnation in the Son, and which gives birth to the primitive Church. In contemplating this supreme gift, he received the spark and the capacity to be a pilgrim of the Church on the roads of his contemporaries. "Wisdom did not only give man his enlightenment in order to recognize the truth, but also a marvelous ability to make him known to others.... He gave Moses the power to speak clearly.... He gave his words to the prophets in order to remove, destroy, dissipate, build, and plant.... It was Wisdom who gave the apostles the facility to preach the Gospel everywhere and to proclaim God's marvels.... He made their mouths become a treasure of words" (ASE 95).

In his heart-to-heart with Wisdom, Louis Marie would allow him to work in him and be led by him, and, in that way, he would be pushed to take an effective part in the compassion of God. For, how can one love Wisdom without imitation, without "coming as close to man as possible and giving them tangible witness to his love?" (ASE 70). What meaning is to be given to a consecration to Jesus through Mary if this radical abandonment does not find its result and bounty in an impassioned missionary commitment to the glory of God? Is it not from the glory of God that man will be saved? "If I didn't have the hope which you granted to this poor sinner in the interests of your glory…I would absolutely pray with a prophet: '…take away my life' (1 Kings 19:4)" (PE 14).

We can ask ourselves what meaning we have given to the glory of God and pray a psalm of praise (96). Louis Marie was profoundly imbued with God's dream for man, from this God "…who saw the misery of (his) people…knew their suffering… and who came down to deliver them…" (see Ex 3:7–8). He felt he was granted a salvific mission which went beyond him and projected itself into the heart of the painful realities of his time. He understood that all human initiatives to the service of the world revealed the mercy of God. Today, it is in the same movement of seeking Wisdom, in this same mysticism of attention to our underprivileged brothers and sisters, with the same obedience to the Church that Louis Marie invites us "to work our field." With him, let us ask to believe in the grace of "the gift," and to distance us from all temptations to stray from the mission.

Louis Marie had the conviction that "to make Jesus Christ known" was of great urgency in the seventeenth century. "The holy Church was truly made to say: '…yet the world did not know him (Jesus Christ)' (Jn 1:10), Incarnate Wisdom; and, to sanely say, to know what our Lord endured for us and not ardently love him as the world does, is something morally impossible" (ASE 166). His profound intuition which we must make known in order to make it loved would inspire a missionary strategy of proximity: he would go out "to meet it."

In his time, the idea of a Church made up of "the people of

God," this presence of people as constant in the Old Testament as in the time of Christ, seems to be completely removed from the truth. However, for him, spiritual salvation could only be sought and found in the Church. Christians don't have to retire into a secure individual piety, but rather to "acquire the light and necessary balm, to inspire others with the love of Wisdom, to lead them to eternal life" (ASE 30). Louis Marie asks us to expose ourselves to the light of Wisdom, let his rays shine on us in prayer, listen to his words and let them penetrate into our hearts, let ourselves be transformed into him in order to be able to transmit a spark of his love to others. "The words that divine Wisdom gives us are not communal, natural, and human words; they are divine words.... They are words that are strong, touching, penetrating...which come from the heart of the one through whom he speaks and go all the way to the heart of the one who hears him" (ASE 96).

Today, after two thousand years of evangelization, the Church can still say "that the world doesn't know him." Through Vatican II, Christians are called to re-hear the call. We are all called to holiness and, by virtue of our baptism, called to participate in the mission. In this era, there are numerous paths that open to those who are seeking...but many expose themselves to the abuses of false hope and so few recognize the one who told us: "I am the way, and the truth, and the life..." (Jn 14:6). Now, at the beginning of the third millennium, Louis Marie appears to us to be a model for the new evangelization. With him, we can ask for the passion of the Gospel and the capacity to enter into a new dynamic adapted to the needs of the hearts who await God.

We can also ask for the protection of those who, like Louis Marie, have made our Lord known and loved.

The Christian, paternal love that I have for you is so strong that I will always carry you in my heart, through life, death, and for all eternity! I would rather forget my right hand than forget you, no matter where I am.... Remember then, my dear children, to ardently love Jesus Christ, to love him through Mary, and everywhere and before all, make your true devotion to the Most Blessed Virgin, our good Mother, burst forth in order to belong to Jesus Christ, to constantly carry your cross like him, and to win the crown and the kingdom that awaits you. Thus, you will faithfully fulfill and practice your baptismal promises...say your rosary every day...and frequent the sacraments (LM 1, 2).

REFLECTION QUESTIONS

In what ways do I evangelize in my daily life? Do I speak up (and speak the Gospel) in situations that cry out for truth and loving response? Am I frightened or embarrassed to speak in the name of God? Might I pray for the grace of courage in my spiritual endeavors? Do I respond to difficult people in a loving manner, that they might be transformed by the power of love in the face of hate or indifference?

DAY THIRTEEN

To Give Us Proof of His Love, Wisdom Chose the Cross

FOCUS POINT

The human mind, as limited as it is, cannot understand the meaning of the cross completely. It is beyond our human capabilities. This we do know: God chose the cross in his wisdom as the trophy for the triumph over death. We celebrate it thusly, and embrace the cross in our own lives, in our own suffering. We are united to Christ by his cross, by his willingness to embrace our human suffering and accept the death that came with the cross. By the cross, there is victory over death, and union with God has overcome the final obstacle.

This is what I believe...the greatest mystery of Eternal Wisdom, the cross. Oh, how distant are the thoughts and paths of Eternal Wisdom from those of man, even the wisest! God wants to redeem the world, render infinite glory to the eternal Father. That is a great plan, a great undertaking. In what way will Wisdom work? With a single flick of the wrist, he could destroy and create what he wants; with a single word from his lips, he could negate and create, what do I say? He only has to will it in order to do anything.

But his love provides rules for his power. He wanted to be incarnated in order to give man witness to his love; he wanted to descend to earth, himself, so that he could lift man to the heavens. But this incarnate Wisdom appeared glorious, without poverty, without humility and weakness, he wins man's hearts with his charms, pleasures, grandeurs, and riches.

Nothing less than all of that. That is something amazing! In the Jews, he sees scandal and horror, and in the pagans, an object of foolishness, a gibbet, or a cross. It is this cross on which he throws his eyes; he takes his pleasure there; he cherishes it...to be the instrument of his conquests, the friend and spouse of his heart. O depth of Wisdom and knowledge of God! How surprising your choice is, how your plans and judgments are...incomprehensible! But how unutterable your love for this cross is!

Wisdom loved the cross... (see ASE 167, 168, 169).

"For God's foolishness is wiser than human wisdom, and God's weakness is stronger than human strength" (1 Cor 1:25). Louis Marie had experienced the foolish love that God had for man, manifested in weakness and vulnerability.

He considered the Incarnation to be "the first mystery of Jesus Christ"—"mystery" in the sense of an event in the life of the Savior—he saw a summary there of all of the others, enclosing "the will and grace of all" (VD 248), making them possible. Through the Incarnation, Christ chose to share everything about the human condition, except sin, to join man in work, suffering, and death. The redemptive Incarnation was God's preferred path.

Crucified, Christ completely revealed trinitarian love. Just like at Jesus' baptism and the Transfiguration, the Father loved himself through the incarnate Word, with an unutterable love. "This is my Son, the Beloved; with him I am well pleased; listen to him!" (Mt 17:5). The crucified Son loved his Father with the same love of which he loved him eternally (see Jn 14:31). The Father could not love his Son without loving him in his human condition of suffering. He made him his prophet. The Son, in this same condition as a "suffering servant," welcomed the loving will of his Father and manifested it to the world. It is thus that the Holy Spirit, the reciprocal love of the Father and Son, could be given to man.

For it is truly in man that God wanted to manifest and send his love. "Through his infinite charity, he (the Son) was made our security and mediator next to God" (VD 85 and 87). He chose suffering and death on the cross to unite with man in his suffering and death, and express "a greater love" (ASE 164).

"No one has greater love than this, to lay down one's life for one's friends (those people he loves)" (Jn 15:13). Lord, you said it and did it. Thank you for revealing your Father's foolish love to me: "Whoever has seen me (on the cross) has seen the Father" (Jn 14:9). I believe that you are in the Father and he is in you. The summit of your suffering is the supreme expression of your love. O cross, you are my only hope!

"Wisdom loved the cross!..." Wisdom or foolishness? Jesus Christ, Eternal Wisdom, would have been able to touch men's

hearts and easily triumphed over evil "without poverty...humility and weakness" (ASE 168). He decided otherwise, renounced "the joy that was set before him (and) endured the cross..." (see Heb 12:2). His choice shook up worldly
wisdom which was denounced by Saint James (see 3:13–17)
and confirmed the upset of the values proclaimed by the beatitudes. And God did not change. The covenant between Jesus
and the cross was indissoluble. He espoused it, he identified
with it. It was, then, from that time on, impossible to find
Jesus without it: "Never the cross without Jesus nor Jesus without the cross." "True Wisdom (Christ)...dwelled so much in
the cross that, outside of it, you will in no way find him in this
world, and he is so incorporated and united with the cross,
that we could truly say that Wisdom is the cross and the cross
is Wisdom" (see ASE 170, 172, 180).

"This teaching is difficult" (Jn 6:60). And yet the Lord is
the one concerned with your life and death. You want neither
evil nor suffering since you created man for happiness. But,
apparently powerless in the face of evil, you wanted to be in
solidarity with all who felt they were incapacitated by pain.
On the cross, you made yourself become "the good Samari-
tan" for man in his misery, taking upon yourself all suffering
(see Isa 53:3, 10). Only love can reveal the meaning of your
"annihilation." From then on, nothing could separate us from
you. You taught us how to love right to the end (see Jn 13:1),
to excess (see ASE 64, 70, 155), by remaining with the cross
(ASE 171), by dying there for us, even if we were still sinners
(ASE 156). Your cross opens the true road to happiness for us,
the one of the total gift to the Father and man. "During the
lives of the saints / They sought only the cross / It was their
great desire / That was their choice" (C 19, 15). The saints
understood the cross. Just like you, they welcomed their own

every day as being good and precious. They loved it throughout the entirety of their life, like an indispensable tool through which the Divinity entered man. Give me a little of their wisdom in order to enter into this mystery and understand that, if there is an excess, it is first on your side, an excess of love.

Louis Marie spoke little of the Resurrection. Jesus' suffering and death on the cross did not constitute an ending for him. Just like the authors of his era, he celebrated "the triumph of eternal Wisdom in and through the cross" (ASE, chap XIV). "Was it not necessary that the Messiah should suffer these things and then enter into his glory?" (Lk 24:26; see Phil 2:8–11).

The cross is a trophy for a victory that is worthy of adoration. On the day of judgment, Wisdom "will have the angels carry this cross in triumph, who will sing canticles of joy. He will follow this cross, placed on the most striking cloud that ever appeared, and will judge the world with and through it" (ASE 172). Here, Louis Marie brings back an idea that many Fathers of the Church expressed, especially Saint John Chrysostom.

In the meantime, the glorious cross is the rallying sign for the soldiers of Christ to steal from victory to victory (ASE 173), since the "crucified Christ" has become "the power of God and the wisdom of God" (1 Cor 1:24). His triumph is not purely eschatological—theologically concerned with death and destiny; it manifests itself here for peace. The gentleness of Christ is, above all, interior joy: "I am overjoyed in all our affliction" (2 Cor 7:4).

Louis Marie was at a loss for words to explain this joy yet he spoke of it like an expert. He wrote: "If we can imagine all of the greatest joys here on earth, the joy...of a poor person that we fulfill with all sorts of wealth; the joy of a merchant who makes millions; ...the joy of the army generals who bring victories; the joy of the captives...delivered from their irons," all of these joys are small in comparison! The joy "of a person who is crucified, and who suffers includes and surpasses all of them" (LAC 34). The knowledge of the crucified Christ makes us discover that the way of the cross becomes a way of joy in as much as we walk it with love: "We know that we have passed from death to life because we love one another" (1 Jn 3:14).

O cross...I did not know you at all,
Forgive my sin.
Dear cross...I give you my heart...
I take you for my life...
my only happiness...
Imprint your grace,
On my heart and arm...
On my forehead and face
It will not make me blush...
For my wealth I will take
Your rich poverty...
For your tendernesses I will take,
Your gentle austerity...
May your wise foolishness
Be, for my entire life,
Glory and splendor... (C 19).

REFLECTION QUESTIONS

How has my perception of Christ and his cross changed as I have grown in my spiritual life? How has my perception of the crosses I encounter in my daily life changed as I have matured? When I am suffering in some way (physically, emotionally, or spiritually), do I reflect on the cross, on Christ's own pain and suffering that I read about in the Gospels? How does this affect the way I view my own suffering? Might I begin to view periods of suffering in my life as "graced moments" that can bring me closer to God in love?

DAY FOURTEEN

Students of a Crucified God

FOCUS POINT

In real love, we are called to die to every attachment in our lives so that God may be loved to the fullest. The image of the cross is our symbol of detachment. Just as Christ gave up his life for the salvation of mankind (because our Creator loved us so much and wanted no more that we be separated from him by the sin of death), so must we die to our selfishness, that we become fully united to God by giving in to his divine will. We must seek to abandon ourselves in search of our God; we cannot be tied to our selfish wills if we are to be truly united to God.

Friends of the cross, students of a crucified God, the mystery of the cross is the great mystery you must learn in a practical sense in the school of Jesus Christ, and which you can learn nowhere other than in his school. The one amongst you who knows how to better carry his cross, when he doesn't know his ABC's, is the wisest of all.

If you know to suffer joyously, you know more than a doctor in the Sorbonne, who doesn't know how to suffer as well for you (LAC 26).

You are members of Jesus Christ, what an honor! But what a necessity to suffer for this quality! The Head is crowned with thorns, and the members will be crowned with roses? The Head is scoffed and covered with mud on the road to Calvary, and the members will be covered with perfume on the throne? The Head has no pillow on which to rest, and the members will be delicately put to sleep in a soft bed, under a feather quilt? That would be monstrously outrageous.... It is necessary for the disciple to be treated like the master and the member like the Head (LAC 27).

You do not know that you are the living temples of the Holy Spirit, and that you must, like so many of the vibrant stones, be placed, by this God of love, into the building of the heavenly Jerusalem. Therefore wait to be shaped, cut, and chiseled by the hammer of the cross; otherwise, you will live like the rough stones that are used for nothing, that we scorn and throw far away.... Perhaps this skillful and loving architect wants to make you one of the first stones of his eternal building, one of the most beautiful portraits of his heavenly kingdom. Let him then do it; he loves you, he knows what he is doing, he has experience at it; all of his strokes are adept and loving, he makes no false moves if you don't make them by your impatience (LAC 28).

In the parishes where he preached, Louis Marie invited the people to join the Association of "The Friends of the Cross." The long letter written for this purpose—the above texts are extracts—seeks to stimulate their perseverance, following a conversion that happened during the mission. Each page of this letter is nourished with the Word of God, beginning with the Gospel of Saint Matthew (16:24): "If any want to become my followers, let them deny themselves and take up their cross and follow me."

It is a necessity for all Christians to carry their cross. "All of us who have been baptized into Christ Jesus were baptized into his death...so we too might walk in newness of life" (Rom 6:3–4). The difference between the "old" and "new" man, the "flesh" and the "spirit" is the source of renunciation and suffering. The cross is one logical consequence of baptism: we, everywhere and always, carry the suffering and death of Jesus in our body, so that the life of Jesus would, also, be manifested in our body (see 2 Cor 4:10). According to Saint Paul, that is a daily paschal mystery!

The perspective of the Incarnation, which was dear to Louis Marie, led to the same conclusion: "God the Son wanted to be made manifest, and as it were, incarnate every day in his members" (VD 31). For that, Jesus invites those he has chosen as his "firstborn" to use his same path. "If you are driven by the same spirit, if you live the same life as Jesus Christ, expect nothing other than thorns, for it is necessary for the disciple to be treated like the master, and the member like the Head" (LAC 27). We unite with Saint Paul and Louis Marie's baptismal "contract of the covenant": "I give myself completely to Jesus Christ...in order to carry my cross, as he did, all the days of my life" (OC, p. 826). The more our love for Christ grows, the more the cross will take root in our heart.

There is no need to seek extraordinary crosses, except those who have a special vocation in the Church. To receive oneself from God is to accept oneself with both our riches and limitations, to live in obedience and faith, which is not automatic. Humility, personal discipline in time management, and voluntary limitations in the possession and use of goods, are always necessary. In each day, to reserve a time for prayer and work to keep it, is a never-ending battle. Trials that are personal, familial, and social are always present at various stages of life, inviting us to make choices and then renunciations, in order to constantly re-orient our path in the way of Christ. To feel old, diminished, dependent, more or less abandoned by those who are healthy and active, is often the ultimate purification to which each Christian is asked to consent to through love.

A relationship with another person is not the least cross offered to the disciple. Renunciation of it is the foundation, since we must consider all men as another self, love him as he is, put our self at his service. And even more between those who are baptized, whose only law is Jesus' commandment: "Just as I have loved you, you also should love one another" (Jn 13:34). This is a terrible "just" which goes all the way to the gift of one's life, by consenting to always take the first step again. A requirement of reciprocity that asks for a constant abandonment of self is to mutually welcome, to help, and, each time it is necessary, to reconcile.

Jesus, I am your disciple. Help me to not yield to the temptation of an easy route, to not deliberately leave aside the roughest words in your Gospel (see Mk 14:33; Jn 12:27; Lk 6:21). Mary, your Mother, our Mother, the first of your disciples, had a "heart pierced with a sword." You let her live her pain right to the end, all the way to the base of the cross where she gazed on you above her. She lost everything by losing you, but in that way, became the mother of all the living; grant us, through her, the wisdom to understand the fruitfulness of love during times of trial and abandonment. Help us accept losing everything and to say thank you!....

Each of us carries "his cross and not that of another," a cross made to measure, in a way, even if it always appears to be too heavy: a cross, through wisdom, "you have arranged by measure and number and weight" (see Wis 11:20). Louis Marie commented: "May he carry it! And not drag it!...may he carry it without impatience, without complaint, nor conscious murmuring, without...natural caution.... May he put it into his heart through love...since there is nothing so necessary...than suffering something for Jesus Christ" (LAC 9–10).

For man, the cross remains an insufferable obstacle. How many Christians, confronted with a trial, suffering, uselessness, or a failure, blame God? However, at the heart of the insufferable, the cry of the believer could identify itself with that of the crucified Christ and change itself, as an offering and in love, for all humanity. With respect to powerless mankind turning to God, only a loving presence, often silent and compassionate—in the strongest sense of the word—is liable to help him assume his existence, purify his own representations of God, find hope again by discovering a new meaning for his life, detach himself from the accessory in order to center himself on what is essential.

The suffering of others never leaves the Christian indifferent, whether it takes on the face of an illness, indigence, injustice, or oppression. Christ continues his passion in his members, even if they are not conscious of it: "I was hungry, naked, a prisoner, a stranger..." (see Mt 25:44–45).

The Christian is invited to associate the mysticism of the cross with the battle against evil. He can, in so much as he enlightens his own life with the paschal mystery and the Word of God which give it meaning.

> "If any want to become my followers, let them deny themselves and take up their cross and follow me" (Mt 16:24). Would you scorn poverty in order to run after wealth; avoid pain...to seek pleasure; hate humility...to seek honors? I appear to have many friends, who protest and say they love me and who, really, hate me because they do not love my cross, many who love my hospitality, very few who love my crosses (LAC 11).
>
> I give myself completely to Jesus Christ through the hands of Mary in order to carry my cross as he did, all the days of my life (CA, see OC, p. 824).

REFLECTION QUESTIONS

Do I see the cross as a challenge in my life? Do I see it as a goal for which I strive, as a sad reminder of Christ's death, or as something to avoid? Do I seek to unite myself with the cross? Do I attempt to detach myself from those attachments that keep me from loving God with all that I am? What habits might I pray to abandon (by the grace of God) in the coming weeks? How will abandoning these habits help me to rely more on God and open myself deeper to his abiding love?

The Rose Is the Queen of all Flowers, the Rosary Is the Rose of All Devotions

FOCUS POINT

We honor Jesus, God the Father, and the Holy Spirit by honoring Mary as we pray the rosary. Mary is a glorious model of detachment. She abandoned her will for that of the Father's so that the Son might be born of her womb. May we all seek such self-abandonment in our own lives, that God will find a home in our hearts and souls, and use us as instruments of his divine will. May we unite in saying the rosary so that the Trinity will be honored by our devotion to the Blessed Virgin.

For myself, I find nothing more powerful to draw the kingdom of God and Eternal Wisdom into myself than to unite vocal and mental prayer, by reciting the holy rosary and by meditating on the fifteen mysteries that it contains (ASE 193).

As for myself, I have learned, through my own experience, about the force of this prayer to convert even the hardest of hearts. I have found some where all the most terrible truths preached in a mission have made no impression and who, on my advice, have undertaken the habit of reciting the rosary every day: they have made a conversion and given everything to God (SAR 113).

It is a holy practice that God, through his mercy, established in the places where I have given missions, in order to preserve and increase the fruit... (SAR 135).

Dear reader, through your experience, if you practice and preach this devotion, you will learn more than in any book... (SAR 114).

In this fifteenth day of prayer with Louis Marie, let us allow ourselves to be guided by him. In his school, let us learn to say "the rosary or at least a chaplet" in honor of Jesus and Mary.

In his book, *The Admirable Secret of the Rosary*, he described the richness and manner in which to "recite" it. He principally did it by telling of his own experience and by transcribing long passages of spiritual authors, notably the "Mystical Rose Bush" of the Dominican, Antonin Thomas.

"The rose is the queen of all flowers, in the same way, the rosary is the rose and the first of all devotions" (SAR 25). To abandon it for other prayers would be to let "the source" and "the clear water" "to run after the streams" (SAR 38).

THE OUR FATHER

When we recite this admirable prayer we capture the heart of God by calling him by the name Father. "Our Father," the most tender of all fathers, all-powerful in his creation, infinitely good in the Redemption. God is our Father, we are all brothers and sisters, heaven is our home and inheritance. Is there not something there to inspire us, at the same time, the love of God, love for our neighbor and the detachment from all earthly things? Then, let us love such a Father and say to him, "Our Father who art in heaven...."

"...Give us this day our daily bread." Using the word "bread," we ask what is simply a necessity for life, what is superfluous is not understood.... We ask for it "this day," that is, we are stuck on the present day for all our concerns, relying on Providence for tomorrow. We ask for "our daily bread," thus recognizing our needs which are constantly being reborn and showing the continual dependence we have on God's protection and help (SAR 39 and 40).

HAIL MARY (OR THE GREETING OF THE ARCHANGEL AT THE TIME OF THE ANNUNCIATION)

Through this angelic greeting, God made himself man, a Virgin became the Mother of God, sin had been forgiven, grace had been given to us, man had obtained eternal life.... The angelic greeting is the rainbow, the sign of clemency and grace that God made to the world (SAR 44 and 45).

We praise God the Father because he had so loved the world, that he gave his only Son as the Savior. We bless the Son because he descended from heaven to earth, because he made himself man and because he redeemed us. We glorify the

Holy Spirit because, in the womb of the Virgin, he formed this very pure body which had been the victim of our sins (SAR 46).

If the angelic greeting renders glory to the Holy Trinity, it is also the most perfect praise we could address to Mary.... By each "Ave Maria," you render to Mary the same honor that God gave her by greeting her with the archangel Gabriel.... Saint Bonaventure said: we greet Mary with grace if we greet her with the "Ave Maria" (SAR 48 and 52).

Heaven is in a state of joy, the earth in admiration, each time I say: "Ave Maria..."; I have God's love for her in my heart, when I say: "Ave Maria"; my fears fade...when I say: "Ave Maria"; I find compunction when I say: "Ave Maria"; my hope affirms itself when I say: "Ave Maria"; my spirit rejoices, my grief dissipates when I say: "Ave Maria..." (SAR 55).

THE MYSTERIES OF THE ROSARY

The rosary, without the meditation of the mysteries...for our salvation, would be almost like a body without a soul... (SAR 61).

Like...a painter puts the original before him in order to sketch a portrait more naturally, and at each stroke of the brush he gives, he looks at it. In the same way, the Christian must always have the life and virtues of Jesus Christ before his eyes, to say nothing, think nothing, do nothing that does not conform to it.... Saint Gregory of Nyssa graciously said that we are painters. Our soul is the waiting canvas...the original that we must copy is Jesus Christ, the living image who perfectly represents the eternal Father (SAR 65).

If Moses, on behalf of God, ordered the Hebrew people to never forget the benefits with which they had been filled, for an even stronger reason, could not the Son of God command us to engrave in our hearts and always have, before our eyes, the mysteries of his life, passion, and glory, since they are as much benefits of which he has favored us, and by which, he has shown us the excess of his love for our salvation (SAR 67).

The rosary, recited with the meditation of the mysteries, imperceptibly lifts (us) to a perfect knowledge of Jesus Christ; purifies...of sin; inflames with the love of Jesus Christ...enriches with graces and merits.... Happy is the rosary which gives us this knowledge and recognition of Jesus Christ by making us meditate on his life, death, passion, and glory.... We must pass by this easy meditation before lifting ourselves up to the more sublime degree of contemplation.... Do you want to reach a high degree of prayer every day? Say, if you can, your complete rosary or at least a chaplet (SAR 81, 82, 76, 78).

THE WAY TO SAY THE ROSARY

We advise the whole world to say the rosary: to the righteous to persevere and grow in God's grace, and to the sinners in order to get out of their sins... (SAR 118).

It is not properly the length, but the fervor of the prayer that pleases God and wins his heart. A single "Ave Maria" that is well said has greater merit than one hundred fifty that have been poorly said.... We must pay close attention, for God listens more to the voice of the heart that to that of the mouth... (SAR 116, 119).

After having invoked the Holy Spirit, put yourself, for a moment, into the presence of God and make offerings of decades.... Before beginning the decade, stop for a moment to consider the mystery you are going to celebrate...and always ask, through the intercession of the Blessed Virgin and this mystery, for one of the virtues which bursts out the most from this mystery of which you have the most need (SAR 126).

Above all, watch out for the two normal mistakes that practically everyone who says a chaplet or a rosary makes: the first is to not make an intention...the second...is to not have any other intention, once you've begun, but to finish it quickly... (SAR 126).

You cannot recite your rosary without having some involuntary distractions, but you can recite it without voluntary distractions.... With reference to this, believe that God and holy Mary are watching over you.... If you must fight this...do it valiantly (SAR 120, 125, 124).

Of all the ways to recite the holy rosary, the most glorious to God, the most salvific to the soul, is to chant it or to sing it publicly. God loves assemblies.... To his apostles and disciples, our Lord promised that every time there were at least two or three assembled in his name, he would be amongst them. What happiness to have Jesus amongst us! In order to possess him, we must simply assemble to say the rosary (SAR 131).

Recite the rosary often, with faith, humility, trust, and perseverance (SAR 136).

If you do not believe what I am venturing, believe in your own experience (SAR 136).

Why don't you try it right away?

REFLECTION QUESTIONS

Do I pray the rosary on a regular basis? Do I recognize the complete prayer that is the rosary? Do I recognize how saying the rosary honors Jesus by honoring his mother? Have I considered joining a rosary prayer group so as to pray the rosary in a public fashion? Might I make an effort to say the rosary (or one chaplet of the rosary) every day for the next two weeks?

Bibliography

De Fiores, Stefano and Alphonse Bossard. *Jesus Living in Mary: Handbook of the Spirituality of Saint Louis de Montfort.* Montfort Publications, 1995.

de Montfort, Saint Louis. *God Alone: The Collected Writings of St. Louis Marie de Montfort.* Monfort Publications, 1995.

———. *The Love of Eternal Wisdom.* Montfort Publications, 1960.

———. *Secret of the Rosary.* Monfort Publications, 1980.

———. *True Devotion to the Blessed Virgin.* Montfort Publications, 1996.

——— and Helmuts Libietis. *Consecration to Mary: Saint Louis de Montfort's True Devotion: Complete Five-Week Preparation: Prayers, Daily Meditations, Spiritual Guidance, Ceremonies.* Angelus Press, 1999.

Doherty, Eddie. *Wisdom's Fool: A Biography of Saint Louis de Montfort.* Madonna House Publications, 1995.